1 Vargas 2014

THE FASHION DESIGNER'S SKETCHBOOK

Fairchild Books

An imprint of Bloomsbury Publishing Plc
Imprint previously known as AVA Publishing

50 Bedford Square   1385 Broadway
London   New York
WC1B 3DP   NY 10018
UK   USA

www.bloomsbury.com

**FAIRCHILD BOOKS, BLOOMSBURY and the Diana logo are
trademarks of Bloomsbury Publishing Plc**

British Library Cataloguing-in-Publication Data
A catalogue record for this book is available from the
British Library.

ISBN: PB: 978-1-4725-6729-1
           ePDF: 978-1-4742-1306-6

Library of Congress Cataloging-in-Publication Data
Rothman, Sharon.
  The fashion designer's sketchbook : inspiration, design development,
and presentation / Sharon Rothman.—First edition.
     pages cm
  ISBN 978-1-4725-6729-1 (pbk.)—ISBN 978-1-4742-1306-6 (epdf)
1. Fashion drawing. 2. Fashion designers. I. Title.
  TT509.R675 2016
  741.6'72—dc23
                                        2015009860

Cover image copyright: Jessica Smalec

Typeset by Lachina
Printed and bound in China

*This book is dedicated
to Sol*

THE FASHION DESIGNER'S SKETCHBOOK

Inspiration, Design Development, and Presentation

Sharon Rothman

Fairchild Books
An imprint of Bloomsbury Publishing Plc

B L O O M S B U R Y
NEW YORK · LONDON · OXFORD · NEW DELHI · SYDNEY

2 Daniel Roseberry

TABLE OF CONTENTS

PREFACE

The Fashion Designer's Sketchbook is written as an extension of how I teach, with respect for each student's creative growth and individual design ideas. It is intended as a companion text for any fashion design course, as well as a valuable reference for anyone wishing to adapt the sketchbook to their individual design needs. My premise centers on three distinct types of creative sketchbooks, each representing a different phase in the design process. One develops out of the other, moving forward organically from first discovery to research to design development and presentation. This covers a lot of territory, so I've designed it for easy use, following a logical sketchbook progression and workable format. The exercises are timed so they can be integrated easily into your individual way of working for any project.

Starting with *Chapter 1—The Sketchbook*, an abundance of carefully selected sketchbook examples explain concepts, offer creative solutions, and illustrate different ways to approach the making of an original, self-expressive design sketchbook with an individual point of view, one that supports each stage in your creative process.

Chapter 2—Pre-design: Your Inspiration Sketchbook acts as the source book for and prelude to developing a fashion design collection. In freely gathering inspiring images and sketched ideas, creativity and personal resonance are explored, along with individual responses to global culture, fashion heritage, and trend awareness. Sketchbook options, assembly ideas, and fabric archiving are considered. Spontaneous sketching-in-the-moment and exercises focused on clarifying design aesthetic and understanding concept building begin your transition to design process.

Chapter 3—Market Research: Your Design Direction addresses the design plan based on real customer needs and market realities. Through in-store comparison and sketched observation, individual design boundaries are identified and explored. Design plan strategies and elements begin to fall into place, informed by personal analysis of online style collections and trend interpretation. Valuable exercises lead to visualizing your design direction effectively with your aspirational market in mind, through the use of idea and image association, in preparation for the process phase of collection design.

In *Chapter 4—Design Development: The Process Sketchbook*, a collection targeting a specific customer and market is developed and organized through an individually directed sketchbook design process. Various process methods suggest choices in how to translate concept into design and theme using color and fabric. Experimentation in spontaneous design sketching guides the communication of quick thumbnail ideas, spinning off into detail-driven groups. A key section on editing includes strategic thinking, resulting in a cohesively edited collection.

The goal of *Chapter 5—Presentation Sketchbook* is to organize the spontaneity of the design process into a portfolio companion sketchbook. Graphic strategies are explored through a variety of visual styles to achieve aesthetically resonant page layouts and advance individual design story. The introduction of an advanced working sketch ties style and proportion to customer and market aesthetic for professional design team communication. Key exercises and page sequence charting help assure an authentic, standout sketchbook.

In *Chapter 6—Innovative/Interactive Sketchbooks*, the focus is on the personal story and how to merge the best of the sketchbook into a polished portfolio that tells the whole design story. Using the sketchbook as design lab brings the realization that it's all one process, exploring one design vision in the sketchbook portfolio. This part follows the emerging careers of several young designers; their creative process evolves individually by absorbing technology and adapting the sketchbook model in studio. This further opens the dialogue to sustaining design creativity and careers through collaboration and design community.

Concluding each section, both young designers and seasoned professionals in all market levels share their perspectives on the creative process, problem solving, and relevant job search advice. A list of resources relating to each sketchbook process concludes this book.

To extend the wealth of personal stories and sketchbook demonstrations by guest contributors, visit *The Fashion Designer's Sketchbook* online at www.bloomsbury.com/rothman-fashion-sketchbook

3 In Jordan Mayer's process sketchbook, she creates a vivid color story inspired by aerial topographical views. You will see how she brings it to design for portfolio collection on page 123.

3

A sketchbook is entirely personal. Allow it to be that space for you—unfiltered and uninfluenced by anyone else—where you have fun, follow your instincts and document what and how inspiration speaks to you.

—*Cecily Moore,* The Paper Curator

CHAPTER 1
THE SKETCHBOOK

Sketchbooks have existed since before the invention of the printing press, but creative thinking on paper is as old as paper itself. The sketched inventions and drawing explorations of Leonardo da Vinci and Michelangelo come alive for us on their sketchbook pages. We can see the work of Vincent van Gogh and Pablo Picasso evolving through their artistic challenges and learn line quality and technique from the sketches of Henri de Toulouse-Lautrec and John Singer Sargent. As designers, we follow in the footsteps of architects, industrial designers, and couturiers who have used the pages of their sketchbooks to work through different sorts of problems, explore design solutions and explain their unique perspective. We see how each design mind thinks and expresses its aesthetic, from Coco Chanel's daringly practical adaptations to Christian Lacroix's crazy-lush collage process.

Over the last decade, I've noticed a radical change in the fashion design sketchbook as young designers respond to cultural shifts, not just with their fashion style or digital presence but with a more globally aware, creative confidence. My students' inclusive design perspective, their often surprising conceptual interpretations, and their willingness to take innovative and emotional risks have shifted my perception of what a sketchbook can and should be.

1-1 Yena Kim brainstorms photo shoot ideas and web page design for her Tumblr brand launch, Menswear Dog.

1-2 Aquily Arias explores design freely in her sketchbook.

1-3 Giulia Cauti thinks through her design direction in words and imagery.

The fashion designer's sketchbook is about something very personal but ultimately very public—your creative design process. Playing and problem solving are synonymous in design, and the sketchbook is your place to have fun experimenting and taking chances. Here you are free to express your personality, make mistakes, rework your ideas, and figure things out.

> **I don't have a lot of respect for talent.
> Talent is genetic. It's what you do with it that counts.**
> —*Martin Ritt, American director, actor, and playwright*

Telling Your Design Story

The global fashion market responds to change in a heartbeat. Today's design team needs to find fresh ideas quickly, and design directors look to the fashion designer's sketchbook in their search for their next new hire. Calvin Klein, benefactor and mentor of the FIT (Fashion Institute of Technology) capstone collections, advised graduating students recently that their jobs will most likely be won not by digital skills and portfolio alone but also on the clarity and strength of their design sketchbook. CFDA designers agree that the sketchbook provides a quick, authentic, visual overview of the individual candidate's creative originality, taste level, personal aesthetic, and design intelligence—a much more accessible hiring springboard.

1-4 Individual aesthetic: Naama Doktofsky tells her sportswear design story informally, moving color and pattern throughout her quickly sketched collection in rhythmic progression.

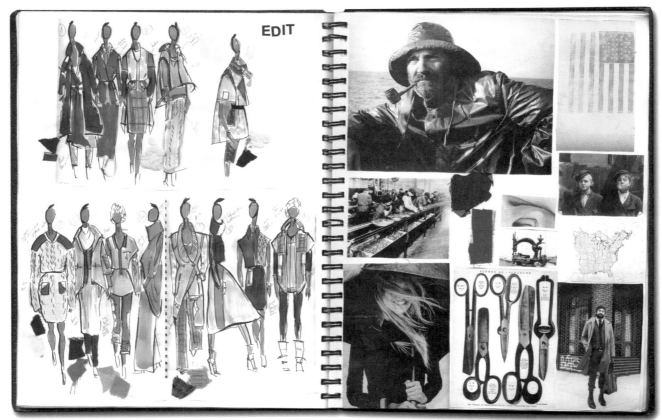

1-4

Designers at all market levels have differing requirements to fulfill when hiring, but they all crave new ideas. They are attracted at first glance by a compatible aesthetic and next by great design. They look for your quick-sketching ability, knowledge of construction, and clarity and organization in communicating your ideas in process. But it is the power of your unique point of view, as presented visually on the pages of your sketchbook, that has the potential to set you apart in the world of fashion design.

So, when it's time for you to organize and present your collection process with your portfolio, your experiments with workable design models and techniques will help you in communicating your design strengths with vision and authenticity.

- Visual metaphor will sharpen your ability to translate your abstract concepts into a clear design message.
- A well-researched market perspective will give you the advantage in targeting your portfolio collection to the design team of your dreams.
- Working sketches will explain your design thinking.
- Editing scenarios will make it easy to achieve a cohesive collection.
- Graphic strategies will show you how to project your aesthetic into a design story that flows in sequential progression.

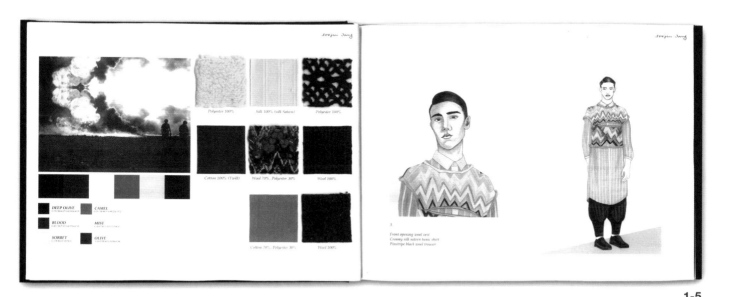

1-5

1-5 Soojin Jang combines the same elements more formally in her innovative menswear design competition sketchbook presentation, clearly expressing her personal aesthetic.

What Your Sketchbook Does for You

Designers at all stages of their careers rely on their sketchbooks to support them in very individual ways and use them to play creatively, evolve design vision, clinch the job, collaborate with a mentor or design team, sell a project for start-up funding, or communicate with artisans and production people half a world away. The sketchbook is a living document, which means that you are continually evolving your design thinking on its pages—editing, revising, and remixing. Like a roadmap, it shows your design journey from first wanderings to collection destination. It records your moments of inspiration and invention and the emergence of your conceptual associations; your key decisions about customer, color, and fabric; and the ongoing development that propels your designs forward to final edit. It keeps you motivated, organized in one place, and on track through the weeks of experimentation and creative choices.

This uniquely individual process is how you grow your creativity and clarify your design ideas, learning your design story from yourself as you experience it. As you do, your sketchbook provides the clearest snapshot of who you are as a designer and what you are saying in your work—a spontaneous "selfie" of how you think design. Take your own best shot.

> " Sketchbook starts as an experiment in following wherever your creativity takes you and emerges as a snapshot of your individual design process. "

1-6 Alexis Yun Young Chung evolves her unique design point of view.

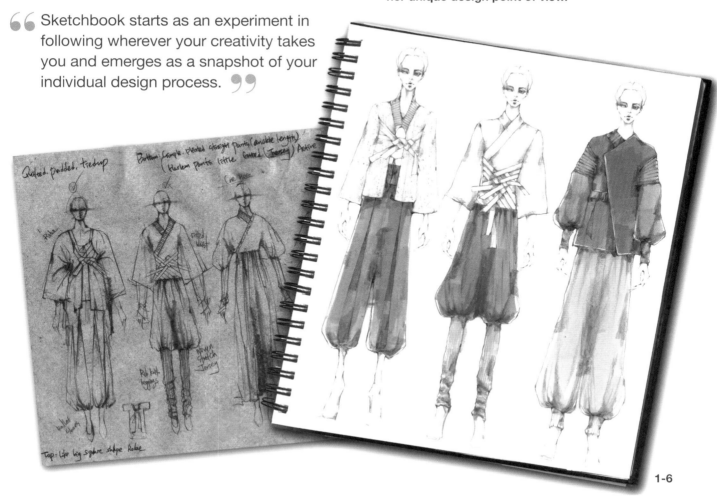

1-6

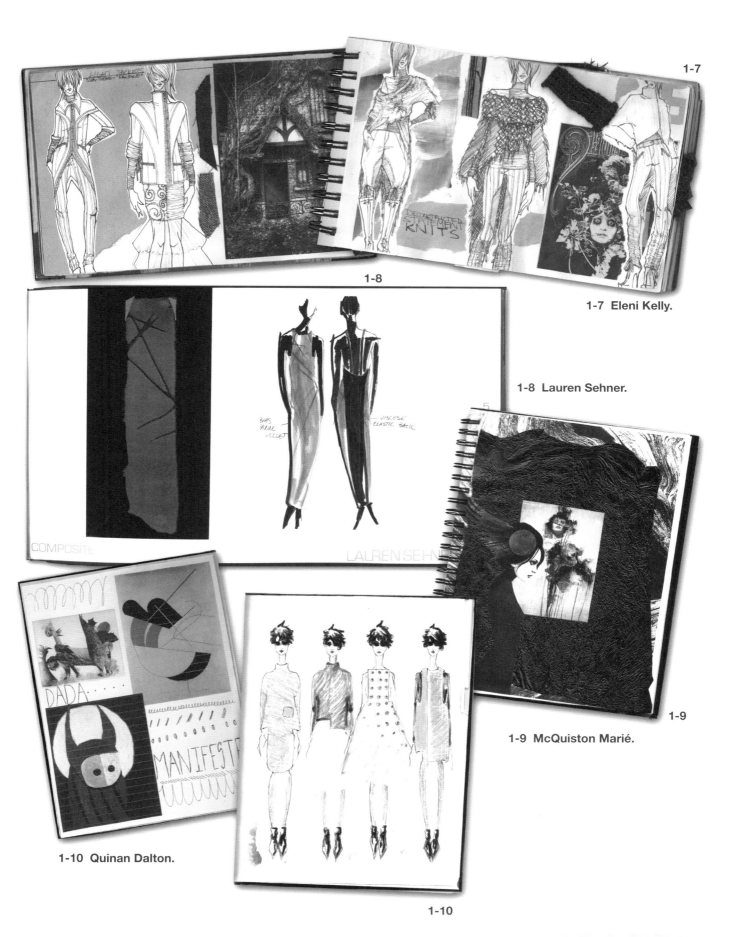

1-7 Eleni Kelly.

1-8 Lauren Sehner.

1-9 McQuiston Marié.

1-10 Quinan Dalton.

1-11

ANDORA WHITFIELD

After graduating with a BFA in fashion design from FIT, Andora worked for a boutique recruiting firm specializing in the fashion industry, with clients in designer, contemporary, and mass markets. During the last four years, she has worked in-house for an iconic American retailer, partnering to lead recruitment for design, merchandising, and supply chain, as well as their college recruitment programs.

> **A sketchbook lets me climb inside a person's head to see what inspires them, and how their design process translates to a finished portfolio.**

From a job search point of view, what do you look for in a sketchbook?

A sketchbook is extremely powerful. It lets me climb inside a person's head to see what inspires them, and how their design process translates to a finished portfolio. It's exciting to see people thinking outside the box, pulling from a lot of different genres for inspiration and including different materials in their sketchbooks. Sometimes the messier the better, because it lets the viewer feel and touch things and get involved in their creative process.

What makes a successful sketchbook?

Spontaneity is really important in a sketchbook. It's your time to let your thoughts flow freely and your ideas come out. You may start in one place, and through that intuitive flow, end up somewhere else. It should be an organic process that allows you to come to new ideas and get your brain working creatively. Everything in your sketchbook should relate to your portfolio or project collections. Focus your process on hand sketching your design development and putting exciting visuals and fabrics together to create a standout collection.

How can students develop their design strengths outside of school?

Internships are an amazing and important way to get started in the industry. Interns are able to participate in meetings, in fittings, and work directly with designers and their cross-functional partners. Interning with a company that you would want to work for also gives you an advantage. The team will get to know you and the value you add. Many companies fill their entry-level roles with interns for just this reason.

What is your most valuable advice for any student?

I recommend that you take advantage of all networking opportunities and that you build strong relationships during your time as an intern. The connections that you make early on are going to be with you throughout your career. It is possible that an internship will transition into a full-time job opportunity—therefore building strong relationships is of the utmost importance.

See Andora Whitfield's video interview online at www.bloomsbury.com/rothman-fashion-sketchbook

1-12 Jenna Polito—portfolio presentation sketch in watercolor. While studying fashion design at FIT, Jenna won the Art Specialization Critic's Award for Design Excellence. She is now an associate designer at a major American retailer.

1-12

1-13

DANIEL ROSEBERRY

A Texas original, Daniel Roseberry began his successful New York design career with an AAS in fashion design from FIT. While there, he won the Art Specialization Critic's Award and, upon graduating in spring 2008, interned in production for an upper-echelon design company. Daniel was quickly noticed by the creative director and, after showing his portfolio, was asked to step in as designer of Men's Collection. After two years, he transferred over to launch Women's Collection and stayed as design director for three years. For the last two years he has been design director for both collections.

How do you start your creative process for runway collection?

About a month before I begin, I'm consciously taking in visual inspiration. I like to "invest in the bank," consciously taking in visual inspiration from anything that is not fashion. Art books on painters are especially inspiring to me, and I spend a lot of time listening to music, which stirs my visual process. By the time I'm ready to sketch, I've already done my intuitive research. I'll devote time to sit, alone and uninterrupted, drawing faces first and trying to get to know her. I let it flow from there, drawing and exploring ideas . . . and then it just kind of happens.

How do you set boundaries and bring your creativity into focus?

I map my thoughts . . . there's nothing visual about this. It's basically just the core ideas in a very navigable map. I write words that could describe a feeling, or be translated into a trim, and when certain elements come up in sketching or in conversation, they go through those filters and take focus around those ideas.

Did you have a sketchbook process for your portfolio?

I kept a sketchbook in my own way . . . a loose-leaf process. But it's lost forever. I do keep most of my concept and process sketches for the work I do now, because I've learned that it's extremely important for design perspective and growth to go back and look at where things came from. But I think the real process for me at that time was the first version I did of my portfolio. I knew that I wanted to leave school and start my career and that this would be my last experimental portfolio from my own perspective . . . and I wasn't feeling good about it. So a week before submission, I re-sketched my three collections, experimenting with watercolors, textural strokes, and line quality. Suddenly it came together and began to express what I was feeling. This is one of the sketches from that portfolio.

See Daniel Roseberry's sketches in *Chapter 5* of this book and his video interview and artwork online at www.bloomsbury.com/rothman-fashion-sketchbook

1-14 Daniel Roseberry—portfolio presentation sketch in watercolor, charcoal and fine-tip marker.

1-14

**My notebook is with me always, always, always.
It is an extension of my mind. . . . I let my mind wander and pay attention
to where it goes. This is . . . how I practice creativity.**
—*Paul Madonna, syndicated artist, "All Over Coffee"*

CHAPTER 2

PRE-DESIGN: YOUR INSPIRATION SKETCHBOOK

Your inspiration sketchbook is a small, unlined diary you carry with you everywhere, sketching your design ideas as you think them, capturing moments of inspiration in words and images. It is your private archive for saving and recording anything you love and everything that gets your creative juices flowing. Independent from the design process sketchbook introduced later in *Chapter 4*, your inspiration diary is dedicated to personal exploration and pre-design research. Here is where your creative ideas are born and your personal vision evolves into design concept.

Throughout your creative life, you will continue to discover and evolve your aesthetic. Keeping a personal sketchbook engages all your senses and gives you the freedom to discover and expand your design horizons. By collecting only the things that have meaning for you, your design voice can speak to you more clearly, and your design choices begin to flow intuitively. As you continue in your career, sketchbook journaling keeps your ideas fresh, communicates your creative intentions, and reinvigorates the fun of designing.

2-1

2-1 Amanda Carlson's irresistible cover image gives her inspiration sketchbook its personality, inviting her to use it every day.

> I am a collector of moments . . . made of images that overlap, that you can't always talk about in a straight line. It is a continuous allusion, pretending that certain things have actually happened.
>
> — *Daniele Finzi Pasca, circus artist,* Donka: A Letter to Chekhov

2-2 Giulia Cauti creates a personal world, layering collected moments into a narrative that inspires design ideas.

2-2

2-3 Brittany Wood crafts her personal journal with ribbons, stitching, and stardust, revealing her natural talent for enchanting children's wear design.

2-3

2-4 Korina Brewer communicates her creative aesthetic through the choice of significant words and images of the 70s rock icon Patti Smith and her technique of torn edges and artfully placed stitches.

2-4

Creativity, Originality, and Inspiration

Creativity is filtered through individual experience and colored by individual imagination. We each see the same thing differently, so your creative potential is uniquely powerful. Your design challenge is not only to think outside the box but also to *create your own box to design within*. Your personal sketchbook is an experiment in defining what your creative box will look like. By collecting and layering your favorite images and meaningful passages, you encourage new ways of seeing and sensing the ordinary. Your research and intuitive associations fuel design ideas. Together they form a creative environment that keeps you inspired and creatively charged and focuses your design explorations into concept and collection.

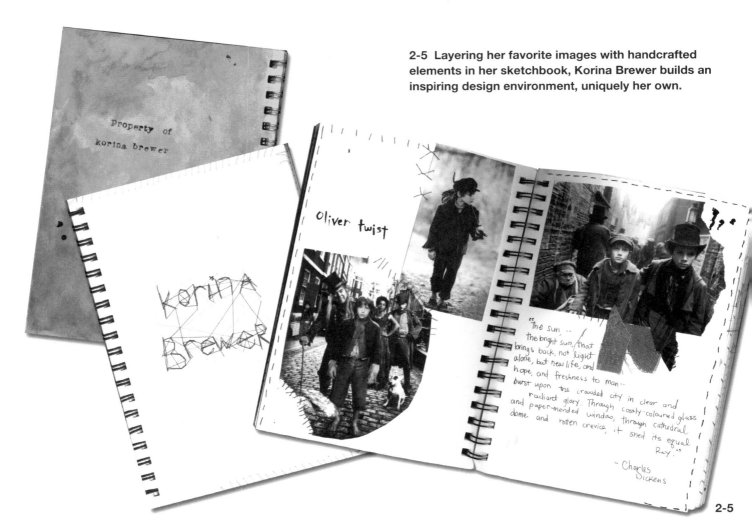

2-5 Layering her favorite images with handcrafted elements in her sketchbook, Korina Brewer builds an inspiring design environment, uniquely her own.

2-5

 Everybody is talented, original, and has something important to say.
—*Brenda Ueland,* If You Want to Write: A Book about Art, Independence and Spirit

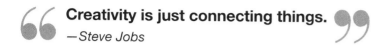

> ## Creativity is just connecting things.
> —*Steve Jobs*

2-6

2-6 Xiao Lin's creative environment explores 1960s modern art as inspiration for design. Her ideas flow intuitively and with originality from her favorite colors and geometric shapes.

Our DNA imprints each of us as an original, but we don't create something out of nothing. We don't create in a vacuum. The designs that are new to you most likely have their roots in the past. This is what Coco Chanel alluded to when she said, "Only those with no memory insist on their originality."

Design creativity requires resourcefulness and a willingness to take risks in putting familiar elements together in new ways. Targeted research, clear intention, and practiced skills are needed to organize and direct the creative process and make your inspiration a reality.

Inspiration

Alexander Sudalnik, designer and fashion journalist, shares his thoughts on inspiration:

"What is 'inspiration' and how do we get 'inspired'? Can only certain people get inspired and only certain things inspire? The Oxford English Dictionary defines inspiration as 'the process of being mentally stimulated to do or feel something, especially to do something creative. *Helen had one of her flashes of inspiration*.' It is also defined as 'the drawing in of breath; inhalation.' Derived from the Latin verb 'to breathe or blow into,' it was originally used in the sense of 'impart a truth of idea to someone.'

"These definitions easily and completely answer the questions above. They strip away any notion of pretense or exclusivity, for inspiration is—at its most basic—the act of living.

"When have you not felt stimulated to do or feel *something*? Whatever people may say, in reality everyone on Earth ceaselessly engages in inspiration—in both its senses. It is not something reserved for the prodigy or virtuoso but actively participated in from the youngest to the oldest person.

"Coming up with ideas becomes easy and simple when you see that you are always encountering inspiration. It's all around you. Keep your eyes open and explore the usual and unusual: environments, places, objects, and people. With this deluge of inspiration, the challenge now becomes deciding which ideas to develop and make your own. Narrowing down options and making decisions can be difficult, but it makes you focus your development and articulate your unique perspective.

"Knowledge of technique and experimentation are invaluable in effectively translating your inspiration into design. You can't use things you don't know, so be sure to learn your craft and its technology! The leaves of a palm frond can inspire the fringe on the edge of a dress, a print on fabric, a layout for a beaded embellishment, or the color palette for a collection. But you have to know what those are in order to use them. Be free in your experimentation and don't reject something before you try it out."

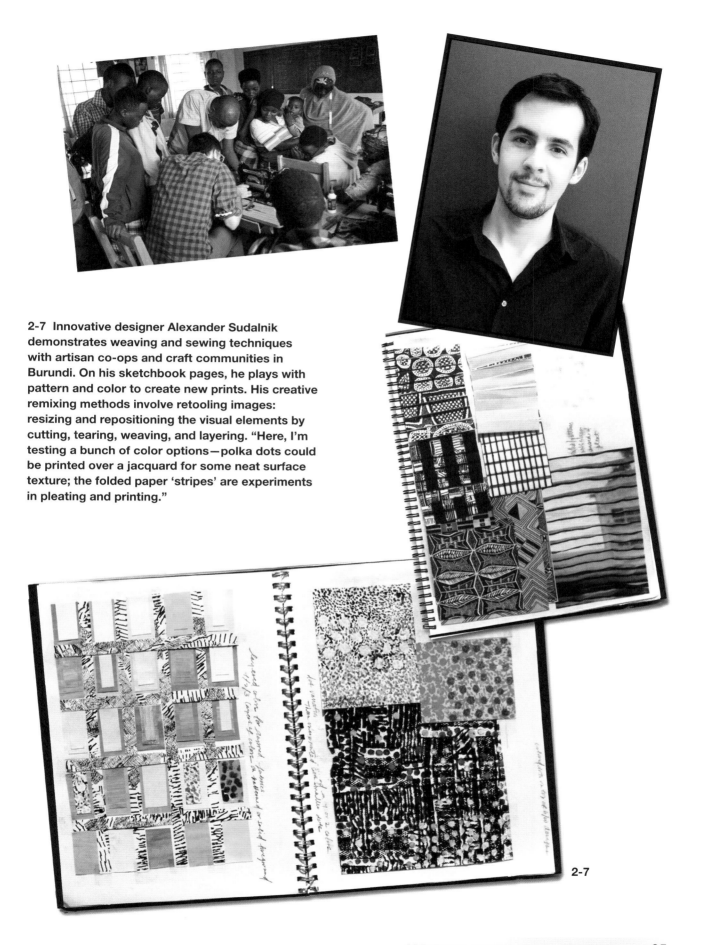

2-7 Innovative designer Alexander Sudalnik demonstrates weaving and sewing techniques with artisan co-ops and craft communities in Burundi. On his sketchbook pages, he plays with pattern and color to create new prints. His creative remixing methods involve retooling images: resizing and repositioning the visual elements by cutting, tearing, weaving, and layering. "Here, I'm testing a bunch of color options—polka dots could be printed over a jacquard for some neat surface texture; the folded paper 'stripes' are experiments in pleating and printing."

2-7

2-9

2-8 Carter Kidd (above) draws design inspiration from his Southern roots. By connecting his quick sketches and notes with visual associations, he begins to tell his design story. For Chanan Reifen (below) everything has print potential, a creative perspective that leads him to experiment in layering visual imagery for a series of original print designs.

2-9 Inspired by the minimalist shapes of American artist Charley Harper, Klara Olsson free-associates shape and color into fashion ideas that reflect her whimsical sense of design.

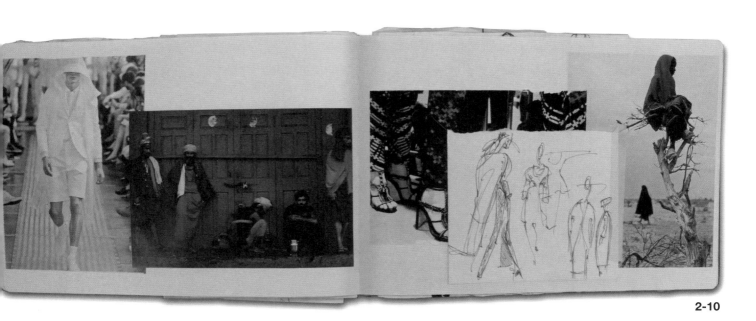

2-10

2-10 Kieran Dallison's directly inspired sketches embody the movement, mood, and contours of his world culture images.

2-11

2-11 "Most of the pictures in my diary I took myself with my smartphone. Additional images are from blogs and such. But I try to create from scratch as much as possible." —Giulia Cauti

The Creative Remix

In *Everything Is a Remix* (TED.com), Kirby Ferguson describes his experience in sound remixing as a contemporary recipe for creativity. "You take existing songs, you chop them up, you transform the pieces, you combine them back together again . . . these aren't just the components of remixing. I think these are the basic elements of all creativity: *Copy, transform, combine*." Your sketchbook facilitates the remixing of visual, tactile, and emotional elements that inspire you. As you immerse yourself in their combined vibe, your natural creative impulse is to "*copy, transform and combine*"—making inventive associations and envisioning other possibilities in what you see. Think of stumbling blocks, constraints, and redos as creative challenges, puzzles to be solved in the remix.

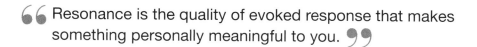

> 66 Resonance is the quality of evoked response that makes something personally meaningful to you. 99

Resonance

Growing up in a culture that constantly floods your senses with random visual patterns and background noise can keep you from hearing your own creative voice. It can be too much and too fast to process into creativity. Learning to be particular about what you allow into your own remix studio and what you allow to pass by is crucial. Resonance makes it easy. Triggered by memory, emotions, and individual sensibility, resonance is the quality of evoked response that makes something personally meaningful to you. When an unexpected image or juxtaposition of colors or shapes hits you, it is resonance that lets you know when your creative connections click. So pay attention to everything, but let your feelings guide your inspirational research, choosing what resonates with you and recognizing the inner associations they arouse.

2-12 The intense fine art images of Benjamin Carbonne resonate with Peter Do's internal story, expressing what can't be put into words, and inspire his award-winning design.

2-12

> ## You can't use up creativity. The more you use, the more you have.
> — *Maya Angelou*

Keeping Creativity Alive

Albert Einstein's famous quote, "Creativity is contagious!" suggests a simple idea. When you surround yourself with images, ideas, and people whose creative energy resonates with yours, it jump-starts your own—the original instant messaging. We keep creativity alive by using it and sharing it. It's a continuous loop, always inspiring more creativity. Seeing how others have approached similar creative challenges and how they view the same ideas and situations, colors, and shapes can inspire new ways of seeing for you.

Nature holds personal resonance with all of us in keeping creativity alive. As our primary source of light, color, sound, texture, shape, and pattern, it inspires when you are out of ideas or feel creatively blocked. Nature's vitality is contagious, recharging your battery and restoring your flow of intuition.

2-13 Marie Heffernan explores beyond the expected design perspective for her Intimate collection, inspired by camouflage ships of the Second World War.

2-13

> **Imagine your eyes are the camera. Place your viewfinder on your shoulder, then on your hip, your foot. Through the shifting lens, you see the same story from different perspectives.**
> —*Will Eisner, originator of sequential art and the graphic novel*

Many artists, writers, and designers trigger ideas by looking at things from different perspectives. Stepping out from your personal frame of reference to see with someone else's eyes is a time-tested approach to problem solving that goes beyond individual creativity. Sometimes we see a problem or roadblock where none actually exists.

Changing the way we see it is the simple answer. By putting together contrasting ideas and images in unexpected ways, you can change the aesthetic or move a storyline further than you imagined. Designing fashion requires a special awareness of where fashion comes from, where it is now, and where you see it going. To do this you need to read the wider pulse of global culture.

2-14 Angélique Chmielewski (left) mixes early twentieth-century style with modern menswear influence. Miguel Pena (right) juxtaposes dissimilar images in a highly individual way to express aesthetic and fuel design.

2-14

CAMINAR POR ENCIMA DE TU PELO...

QUIERO

DARTE UN BESO DE DESAYUNO...

2-15 Paola Bueso-Vadell (left) and Giulia Cauti (right) show they understand their customer's attitude and lifestyle in the images they sketched, or composed on the page.

IT'S MORNING SOMEWHERE

2-15

Who Do You Want to Design For?

How we dress reflects everything about who we are, our place in the flow of time, our cultural aspirations, our tribal status, our individual sense of worth. The designer must learn how to read all this in the way someone dresses and become familiar with the values and preferences typical of different cultures in different eras. It is part of developing your fashion radar. It is also how you begin to read your customer: who she is, what resonates with and nourishes her spirit, and what kinds of clothes she needs for her activities. She will come into clearer focus as you deepen your research into market and customer in *Chapter 3*. Whenever you see the woman you want to dress, the muse who inspires your creativity, clip her photo and sketch her style.

2-16 Using marker line, rough color pencil technique, and a confident attitude, Sharon Rothman imagines the women she wants to design for.

2-16

> ## **We're all creating off each other's cultures.**
> *—Anonymous U.S. musician, 2012 Olympics*

Your Cultural Universe

As one of our richest inspirational sources, culture includes the aesthetics and invention of everything humans have thought, created, preserved, or recorded, to be reinvented and recreated again and again. All designers travel through time to mine the world's treasures for design lines, silhouette, detailing, motif, and color.

Seeking out original source material—the arts, music, architecture, literature, philosophy, costume—for your creative remix inspires original collection design. Rather than retranslating another designer's interpretation, inspired designers dig deeply into the infrastructure of their interest or make personal connections with something outside fashion. Elsa Schiaparelli's originality lay in translating into fashion the surreal vision of her fine art contemporaries with humor and grace.

2-17 Angélique Chmielewski (left) and Jusil Carroll (right) are open to a mix of design inspirations from the global cultural universe, inspiring silhouette, mood, detail, and color palette.

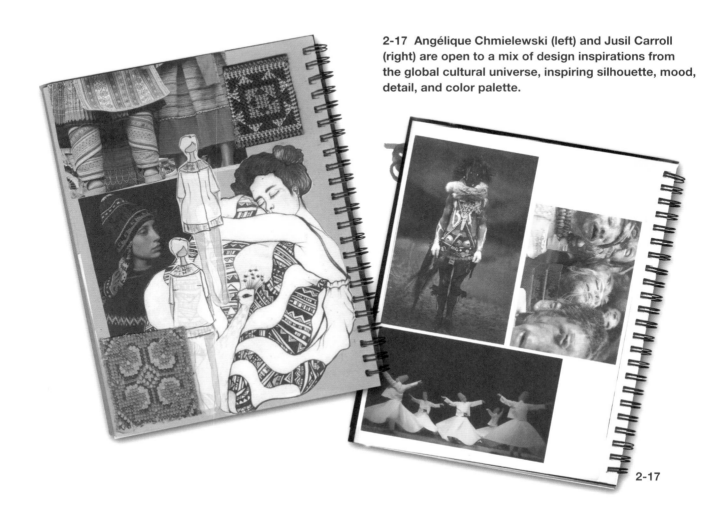

2-17

2-18 Shannon Wagner revisits 1920s Berlin with fresh eyes and finds original source material for inspiration in the innovative Bauhaus style of design.

2-18

 To experiment is at first more valuable than to produce; free play in the beginning develops courage. "
—*Josef Albers, Bauhaus painter/teacher*

Cultural Values

Fashion expresses the cultural values of each successive era, whether repressive or liberating. It preserves the spirit of wisdom from the past, reflects the tipping points of change going forward, and supports your potential to change the face of culture and our evolving human story with your designs.

Inform your design and aesthetic by cultivating your awareness of the history of clothing and psychology of color. As you learn to appreciate the tradition and graceful proportion of Asian dress, you also recognize its power to limit or to dominate behavior. Early twentieth-century designers Paul Poiret and Coco Chanel brought freedom to dressing as Western women won the right to vote and broke out of the culturally imposed modesty and sense of propriety that had so influenced fashion style and taste from the Victorian era. These same values, in the extreme, continue to affect women's lives today in many fundamentally traditional cultures.

Sourcing World Culture

American sportswear is a distillation of the utility and earthy textures of the worker mixed with elements from the international melting pot. Although in many ways American style has become global, each country or region has a distinct design sensibility stylistically rooted in its history that identifies its cultural aesthetic in art and design as well as in fashion. World culture offers an immensely inspirational wellspring of original creativity that stretches design aesthetic beyond the common ground of modern Western style.

World culture and costume history can be sourced in library book collections and picture archives, as well as in periodicals on the arts. Vintage magazines and back issues will supply you with high-quality images of art, architecture, interior design, and fashion that you can easily clip and save with information on each. Experiencing both actual and virtual provides the best possible inspirational foundation for creative design.

 The life of a designer is intimately linked to tastes and sensibilities that change at a moment's notice.
— *PrincetonReview.com*

Trend Awareness

One of the marks of true talent is an intuitive tuning-in to the larger patterns that move fashion forward. Being aware of evolving social trends and their influence over everything from international industry to how women will want to dress next spring adds dimension to your design talent. Staying current means knowing firsthand the creative environment you will be designing in and understanding conversational references to it. Thus you project a

timely vibe into your collection design and develop your cultural intuition. Choose your favorite ways to stay current:

- Keep up with gallery and museum exhibits.
- Check out what's happening in print and online.
- Take in what you can of theater, dance, music, and film festivals.
- Visit cultural centers and library archives dedicated to the arts.

2-19

2-19 Inspired by a visit to the American Folk Art Museum, Giulia Cauti adds inspiring menswear, kimono folds, and fine fabrics to her sketchbook remix for children's wear design.

2-20 Angélique Chmielewski explores regional Asian dress for inspiration, translating its influence into her own design vision and color story.

2-20

Trend Tracking

Li Edelkoort's *Trend Union* is respected by many of fashion's most exclusive design houses. Their social platform *Trend Tablet*'s open access tool describes how trends change over time. It is open to new ideas and invites you to contribute and follow in creative company. Their trend book, *Bloom*, is dedicated to connecting the textures and colors of nature to inspire design, and *Earth Matters* directly connects ideas about transforming overconsumption to sustainability with contemporary design. While such professional trend services provide their seasonal forecasts on color and style only to paid subscribers, *Style.com* and other popular trend sites will keep you up-to-date on the latest runway collections and fashion news free of charge. Whether you make specific use of it or not, trend informs your fashion radar.

Print and Digital Search and Storage

Developing your own perceptions of the world into an individual design vision is crucial for creative design. Insightful use of the Internet can expand your personal culture with inspiring images and designer research. Image bookmarking web sites and social platforms like Pinterest or Tumblr allow you to follow, save, organize, and share the inspirational original works of creators around the world. Make a mental note to always credit the creator of the visuals you pin and use, even in your personal sketchbook—a key practice in ethical sourcing. Image archives are used by millions of creative people with limited time to cultivate their own original sources. Although the images you use may speak to you uniquely, they can quickly become recognizable or dated. So, for truly original sourcing, hit the streets and explore the world with your sketchbook and camera.

Fashion blogs such as The Sartorialist, Style Bubble, or Refinery29 are significant observers of street style and runway and pass along must-read articles from a variety of sources. As a key trade publication in the midst of cultural change, *Women's Wear Daily (WWD.com)* remains a valuable source of fashion industry news, runway picks, and trending style. Fashion magazines such as Vogue and Bazaar influence fashion taste with highly editorialized photo shoots and luxury lifestyle advertising. *Collezione* and *Hola* publish up-close runway shots of haute couture and fashion week collections—a perfect reference for sketching the walking pose and observing how fabric moves with the action of the body.

2-21 Inspired by nature, Xiaonan Gao imagines a fresh, pale color palette for spring design.

2-21

2-22

2-22 With natural graphic awareness, Cecily Moore creates a strong visual effect by combining boldly curving architectural lines with the textures and patterns of nature.

Before I design a woman's wedding gown, I create the story of her wedding day—where it will be held, the season, her dream for herself as a bride. I use Pinterest to compile huge amounts of images, categorize them in precise groups, and select to create my own inspiration boards, like 'Wedding at the Opera' (right). This visual story is my guide and tells me how everything has to feel—the fabrics and the design. It keeps me inspired and grows my client base at the same time.

—Gregory Nato, Fancy Bridal NY

2-

2-23 Designer Gregory Nato creates retro-inspired bridal gowns that fulfill his clients' personal vision and aesthetic, involving them in his design process through visual research.

Setting Up a Workable Image Archive

Whether you research images by skimming through fashion blogs and online image archives or by dedicating time for solitary bookstore browsing, not everything you save will end up in your sketchbook. Here are a few simple tips for setting up a workable image archive:

- In sourcing visuals for your sketchbook, choose high-resolution print images and avoid low-resolution digital images.

- Organize your print tearsheets, book scans, and digital printouts for easy use in folders, just as you would on the computer.
- Keep them sorted as you collect them into design influence categories, such as mood, historical/cultural, shape/silhouette, color, texture, print/pattern, detailing, customer, trending style, sustainability, runway collections, buttons/trims, and so on, getting as specific as you like.

2-24 Gathering allusions from online image sources, Jessica deVries (top) creates a visual narrative to fuel her design story. Feride Ozsoy (center) compiles archived images to make the conceptual connection between art deco patterns and bustier detailing.

2-24

2-25 Ashley Gonzalez selects visuals from her image files as earthy inspiration for autumn sportswear design.

2-25

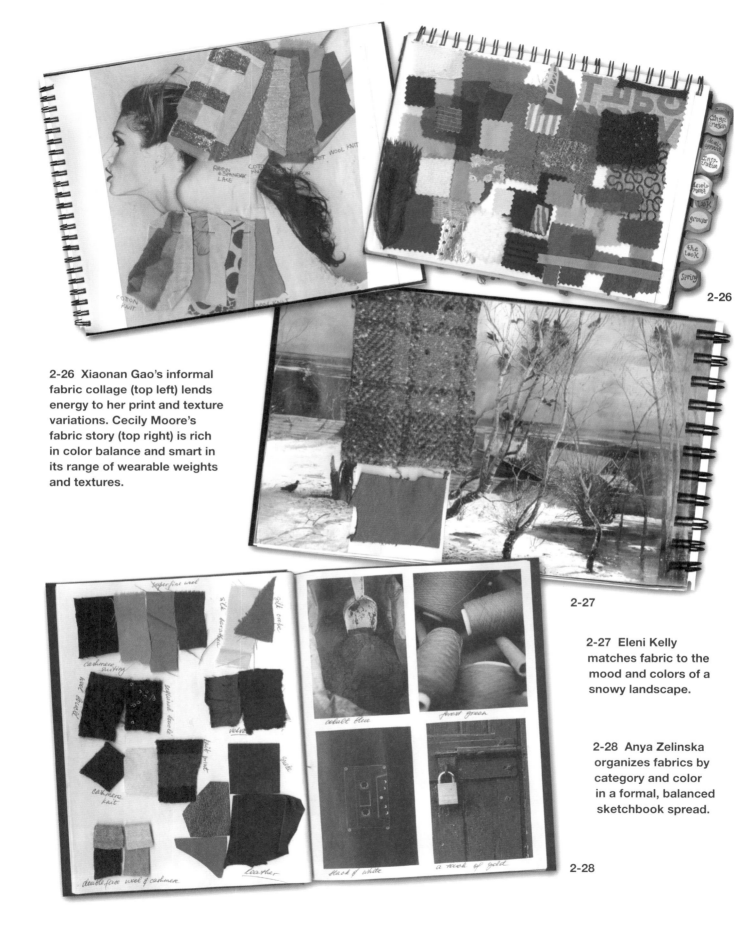

2-26 Xiaonan Gao's informal fabric collage (top left) lends energy to her print and texture variations. Cecily Moore's fabric story (top right) is rich in color balance and smart in its range of wearable weights and textures.

2-27 Eleni Kelly matches fabric to the mood and colors of a snowy landscape.

2-28 Anya Zelinska organizes fabrics by category and color in a formal, balanced sketchbook spread.

2-26

2-27

2-28

Building a Fabric Archive

Textile invention vies with cultural cycles as the key force of change in fashion design. Your creative use of fabric is one of the fundamental ways to set your collection apart from the rest and make even the simplest shirt or pant desirable at any price. The first step to collection for most designers is to attend the key fabric trade shows for advanced design direction. At Premiere Vision or Pitti Filatti, you will find the latest in textile inspiration, trends, and technology to expand your design vision.

Fashion design cannot be approached seriously without a refined sensitivity to fabric quality and knowledge of how different textiles move with the body and hold a manipulated shape. This is information only a trained eye, an educated touch, and experimentation in draping can provide. Always source the highest quality at professional fabric stores, your hands-on research fabric labs, with bolts of yard goods from luxury to high tech and sustainable. Good sourcing relationships are built upon honoring store swatching policies.

EXERCISE 1: Building a Fabric Archive

- Browse, touch, and compare textile quality, hand, weight, and color.
- Choose fabrics that feel right and seem to "design themselves" automatically into your ideas.
- Swatch only the highest-quality fabrics; note name, price, and fiber content of each.
- Collect a large variety of fabrics; organize by name, weight, texture, color, and season.
- Store flat for easy use in clear plastic envelopes, protector sheets, or zip-top bags.
- Visit yarn, trim, button, and bead shops for inspiring textures, colors, and embellishment.
- Experiment by combining or layering swatches with images to tell a fabric story.
- Select a variety of textures and weights of fabrics in colors inspired by one resonant image.

Everything came together for me in my smallest sketchbook. It felt personal and I loved filling each page, watching it get stuffed . . . it's still my favorite.
—*Giulia Cauti*

Putting It All Together

Your inspiration sketchbook should have *attitude*, tempting you to open it with fabric and colors flapping out of its edges. How you fill it is strictly personal. Some put their pages together with confidence and visual focus, sketching directly on pages; others work more carefully or thoughtfully; still others quickly stuff things inside spontaneously, sketching in the moment. Experiment by collaging your images, clearly aligning them, or following your impulse. You will find the technique that feels like the best expression of your design aesthetic.

An inspiration sketchbook is hands on and immediate, so any work that is too studied or refined defeats the purpose. You might crop or enhance your favorite high-resolution images using the computer, but your goal is to get used to the immediacy and imperfection that comes with inspired designing. You will have the opportunity to use digital techniques and controlled layouts later in your process and presentation sketchbooks.

2-29 Luke Hall (left) follows his creative impulse, layering sketches over inspiring research; Korina Brewer (right) combines directional sketch with collage and her trademark quirky stitches.

2-29

Sketchbook Options

Since you will be taking your personal sketchbook everywhere with you, size and weight are essential considerations. It should feel comfortable in your hand and be strong enough to withstand constant use. Choose a small sketchbook ranging in size from 4.5" × 6.25" to 8" × 10", with a standard or spiral binding that opens flat for easy use. However, the smaller the pages, the more difficult it may be to sketch on them. Sketchbooks are available in either vertical (portrait) or horizontal (landscape) orientation. The pages should be bleed-proof and sturdy enough to hold the weight of fabrics and trims.

Methods of Attaching

You may already have your favorite supplies for attaching elements to the page—they are simple and basic. For temporary positioning, use removable tape. When you have everything arranged the way you want it, securely attach your flat images and fabrics using standard double-sided tape, craft roller-applicator with double-sided tape, a glue stick, or single-sided matte transparent tape. For dimensional fabrics and small trims, use a glue gun, stitches, or staples. See Cecily Moore's Supply List in Resources, page 208.

Avoid ruining your favorite images and sketches with the wrong adhesives:

- School paste or liquid craft glues will dry lumpy and brittle.
- Rubber cement can cause marker art to blur or bleed; the toxic fumes require proper ventilation. See Resources for Art Material Safety information.
- Black or colorful tapes divert attention from your images and sketches and can be easily confused with fabric swatches or color chips.

2-30 Strong, black tape dominates Mimi Choi's runway visuals and fine line sketches. Practice drawing correct closures and collar construction, even in your roughest sketches.

2-30

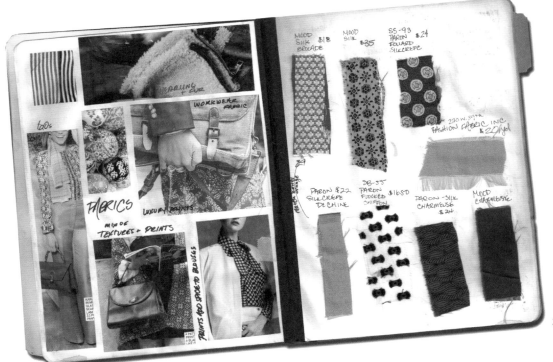

2-31 "It really helped to have my sketchbook with me when I sourced fabric textures and prints for my autumn collection. These images helped keep my color and print choices true to my design plan."
—Amelia Tkach

2-31

EXERCISE 2: Your Own Remix

Keeping a personal inspiration sketchbook motivates you, helps clarify your design vision, and directs inspiration into focused research. These simple steps define your design process:

- Sketch and take photos wherever you go: capture the street style, energy, and movement of the moment and the crowd.
- Search online for inspirational high-resolution photos, art, fashion ideas, trends, and colors. Save them by category in your own digital archive.
- Collect and select inspiring images that can be handled: tear and scan from print sources and print out your digital archive.
- Experiment by making trial arrangements of images, fabrics, sketches, and notes to tell a design story.
- Begin to define your design aesthetic by listing your most meaningful inspirations, for example, Dries Van Notten, batik, Ballets Russes, chartreuse . . .
- Read the next section and choose your sketchbook diary.

2-32 Native American images, colors, and ideas (top) influence Sanly Yuen's natural embellishment and sustainable fabric choices for her design story, "Venerate the Earth." The penetrating lyrics of Neil Young lend an acoustic rock vibe and authentic emotional tension to Jessica Smalec's design story collages (below).

2-32

Creativity happens in your head, but it has to come out and connect to doing—to the process. The first little sketch leads to more expanded versions of your first idea.

—*Claudine Calabrese, Claudine Calabrese Design*

Sketching in the Moment

Sketching is the way designers record their design ideas in the creative moment for later development. Your sketchbook is the perfect place to practice direct sketching when the idea strikes, building confidence as you draw. You will be stretching your capabilities, refining your eye, and defining your sense of proportion. Quick sketching in pencil or pen directly on your sketchbook pages is a challenge for some. Don't think about how to do it, or how it looks, but capture your immediate feelings. The moment you get an idea, don't hesitate—*sketch it*. Keep open the flow of creative impulse from your mind directly to your hand. Adding resonant visuals, swatches, or color chips reminds you of your creative associations and makes for exciting pages.

Your quick sketches are your personal language to yourself, drawn in the way you feel most natural, on figures as flats or rough diagrams. When you draw, practice using enough hand pressure so that your quick pencil sketches are confident and easy to see. Many designers, like Kieran Dallison, sketch over their initial pencil drawings with a fine-tip pen to make them legible and keep their spontaneity intact. Indicate color and pattern with a light touch to avoid a studied effect. Get further tips on process sketching in *Chapter 4* and on the working sketch in *Chapter 5*.

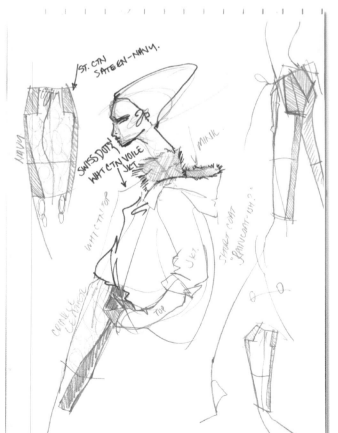

2-33 Kieran Dallison visualizes his design ideas whenever he gets them, "mostly sketching on scraps of paper as I'm getting from place to place, or grabbing lunch."

2-33

2-34 **Spontaneous design sketches by Chanan Reifen (top left); Naama Doktovsky (top right); Luba Gnasevych (center); and Kieran Dallison (below).**

2-34

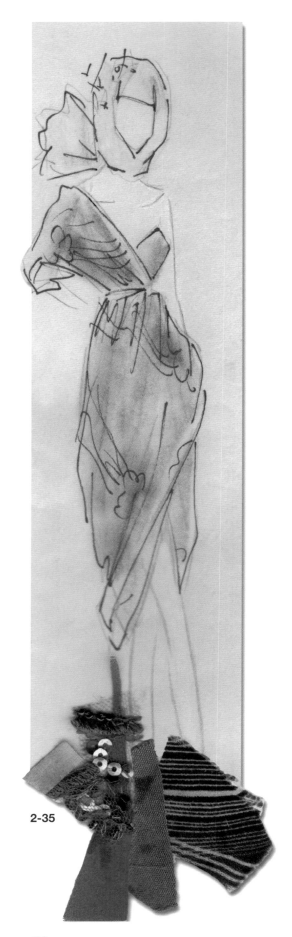

2-35

Sketching Tools and Tips

See Cecily Moore's Supply List in Resources, page 208.

- Choose a fine line pen, medium-soft lead pencil (#2 or 2B), or mechanical pencil that feels comfortable and makes a clean line on your page.
- Black line is most commonly used to sketch fashion, since it acts as a neutral and does not influence or suggest a color scheme.
- Color pencils in black or 90 percent gray allow a nuanced line quality, from thin to thick; for best results, sharpen the points often.
- To show color and texture quickly, color pencils are especially good for soft textural knits, woolens, velvets, or fur.
- Powdered eye shadows work well for indicating soft color. Used with small sponge applicators, they combine with other art supplies and will not bleed through even the thinnest sketchbook paper. Available online in inexpensive sets in colors ranging from black to primary brights, with neutrals perfect for all skin tones.

To avoid a messy sketchbook:

- Pastels, charcoal, and very soft lead pencils smear easily and will imprint onto the facing page. *Lead pencil on tracing paper results in smeared, faded sketches*.
- Brush markers are difficult to control and, until your technique is practiced, can result in heavy-handed detailing. *Experiment using small-nib brush markers for silhouette definition, combined with fine pen line for detail.*
- Alcohol-based art marker colors can dominate your sketch or flood through sketchbook pages. *Try water-based art markers, using a quick hand and light touch to keep it fresh*. See Resources for Art Material Safety information.

2-35 **Meredith Moulton artfully applies powdered eye shadow for color/fabric trials.**

2-36 Quinan Dalton's design explorations (near right) are sketched on folded marker paper too thin for sketchbook use, making them difficult to read. Sanly Yuen's red marker application (far right) floods the garment shape; she preserves her silhouette by leaving space at the edges for defining and detailing with fine line.

2-36

EXERCISE 3: Research Sketching

Visit an upscale department store that sells a full range of fashion apparel, from luxury designer ready-to-wear to contemporary sportswear. Bring your sketchbook and shop with a selective eye. Pay attention to the presence or absence of detail and how colors and fabrics are combined. Feel the quality and hand of the fabrics. Observe the personal style of the customer at the various market levels and price points.

- Choose your favorite looks and sketch the silhouette, proportion, and construction details for each.
- Examine the inside of the garments; read the fabric and price labels.
- Take notes as callouts on each sketch, indicating colors, fabrics, and prices.
- Sketch the customer and find words to describe her.

Transition to Design

Concept is the key to developing a cohesive collection. It generates ideas and helps maintain your focus during the design process. Concept is your framework for what you want your collection to be and should encompass research and market decisions. In your career, it will explain your intentions to a design team, help keep them on track, and provide the press with a way into your creative motivation for the collection.

The answer to finding the concept that is right for you now resides in connecting with your own narrative and following it into a vision for your collection.

Research is to see what everybody else has seen, and to think what nobody else has thought.
—*Albert Szent Gyorgyi*

2-37 "My concept is always my customer—what she does, where she travels, how she reflects style in her own way. For this collection theme, she tours Italy with a backstory of Jackie O. and 1960s Italian style."
—**Amelia Tkatch**

2-37

2-38

2-38 Anya Zelinska's theme visuals for her fall/winter collection are an eclectic mix of primal emotions, ink blot anonymity, and reactive angst, telling her story of "Post Punk" androgynous design.

The essential elements for an easy transition to collection design should now be filling the pages of your sketchbook—source images, fabrics, and sketched ideas for silhouette, color, and detail. Your experimental associations may have already defined your "creative box" into a concept story that you can put into words. Or you may be looking for a way to flesh out a vague conceptual notion that hasn't quite gelled yet.

Decide among your favorite images and colors, fabrics, and shapes that call to you. When placed together, they begin to tell a story that resonates with you emotionally or artfully. Concept can be as straightforward and simple as Amelia Tkach's "Travels to Italy" or take on a more complex narrative with social undertones, like Anya Zelinska's "Post Punk," through which she explores androgyny in her designs.

I like the idea of being a slave to a concept outside of myself. It's kind of like being an actor putting on a character and losing yourself in a role. 99

—*Daniel Roseberry*

Finding Your Design Concept

There are many ways to find a design concept. Both mind mapping and visual storytelling use free association to combine separate or contrasting inspirations into one defined vision. Used alone or in combination, they are powerful tools for focusing your research and collection direction.

Mind mapping uses words in a nonlinear way to trigger free associations and connect different aspects of one central idea. New paths for exploration open up as your descriptive words suggest different combinations of inspiring elements with the goal of creating an overarching visual narrative. This can be an easy way of getting conceptual if you are undecided or stuck as you begin.

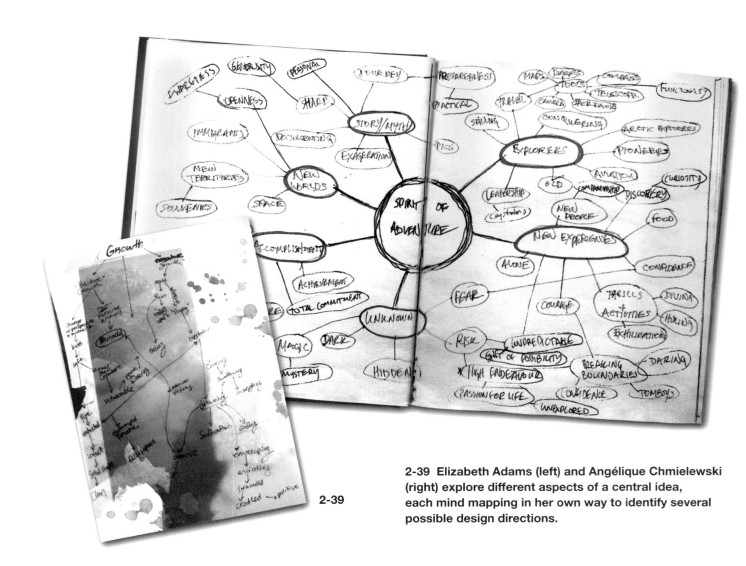

2-39

2-39 Elizabeth Adams (left) and Angélique Chmielewski (right) explore different aspects of a central idea, each mind mapping in her own way to identify several possible design directions.

Visual storytelling is more like daydreaming a concept and theme from various unrelated inspirations, invoking a design story with the potential to encompass divergent design ideas. As you touch, sort, and remix your visuals, layering mood images with silhouette, personal memory with color and detail, your design mind automatically begins seeing new connections through resonant association. These new patterns can create the visual context for your collection, reminding you where you are going as you jump into development.

2-40 Xiao Lin's visual storytelling layers stormy mood and color with folding origami shapes, inspiring her "Geometric Rain" theme for the fall/winter collection.

2-40

> **A concept is more inspirational, directional—it's the mood, the vibe you want the collection to have. The theme can be more practical, inspiring garment details and fabric that then visually translate your concept.**
> —*Naama Doktofsky*

Collection Theme

Think of your theme as the title of the story you intend to tell with your designs. It may emerge naturally out of your concept experiments, as it did for Xiao Lin's "Geometric Rain." Or you may want to let your theme evolve further as you consider your market research, coming up in *Chapter 3*. Either way, your thematic imagery should encompass your intentions for design development, suggesting attitude, mood, color, and season and hinting at your initial design ideas. You may find more than one theme within your concept, as Anya Shakhmeyster did for her critic's award–winning senior thesis collection. Under the broader conceptual umbrella of *surfing*, she united three seasonal collections of easy sportswear: fall/winter "IceSurf," named for the subzero surfers in Siberia; casual resort "NightSurf," named for South Pacific island night surfers; and spring "SolSurf," named for warm water surfers in Brazil.

2-42 "NightSurf."

2-41 Anya Shakhmeyster: "IceSurf."

2-43 "SolSurf."

2-42

2-41

2-43

EXERCISE 4: Visual Storytelling/Mind Mapping

Part 1: Seeing patterns—Initial experiments in concept and theme

- Mind map a central idea and follow new paths of meaning and mood.
- Remix your most meaningful images into a visual story/concept.
- Find a theme or title for your concept; choose words/phrases identifying the attitude, mood, and design ideas your concept/theme contains.
- Try juxtaposing images of contrasting visual/emotional content to create a new direction or version of your story.

Part 2: Remix designing

- Scout for images suggesting silhouette, details, and colors that call to mind your conceptual theme.
- Choose fabrics that express your theme in weight, color, and hand.
- Roughly sketch a few of your design ideas.
- Visualize your concept on your sketchbook pages by combining source inspiration and mood images, design sketches, colors, and fabrics.

The Next Step

Your sketchbook explorations in inspirational research, quick sketching, and the layering of inspired associations with design ideas have led you to conceptual thinking. You have left yourself a very personal trail of breadcrumbs to retrace whenever you get lost in the details, stuck for ideas, or feel creatively blocked by the pressures of time and expectation. The way forward to collection in *Chapter 3—Market Research: Your Design Direction* will shift the role of your sketchbook diary and the focus of your research into the world of market realities.

Read more about visually communicating your concept in *Chapter 4* and *Chapter 5*.

2-44

SCOTT NYLUND

From Owatonna, Minnesota, Scott Nylund made his mark in New York City after graduating from FIT in 2000. An assistant design role at Tommy Hilfiger led him to Beyond Productions, where he advanced to design director for House of Dereon and his spectacularly iconic costumes for Beyoncé's major tours and awards. In 2014, he moved forward into producing his own designs, which are sourced consciously and balance creative design within the world community.

See Scott Nylund's video interview and sketch demonstration online at www.bloomsbury.com/rothman-fashion-sketchbook

How do you use your sketchbook?

I use my sketchbook for almost everything creative, as a diary and a project planner, for random notes and ideas, for all of my research images and sketches. But I also use it to plan photo shoots, sketch out my exhibition design in overview, and work out the display order for each piece in sequence. When I'm working on various projects at the same time, having a different sketchbook per project keeps my information, thoughts, and visual inspiration for one project from getting mixed or confused with another. I always know where to go to find anything related to that project when I need it. I can see the interrelationship of all the elements as I work with them, and select the most relevant images, colors, and mood for my studio inspiration board as I design.

What kind of research inspires your project designs?

I use as much inspiration from primary sources as possible. This way, I'm being inspired by the original and not by another person's interpretation of the subject. By connecting directly and energetically from my own experience, I can interpret what I see however I want. I look for actual photos, not fashion photo shoot recreations. When I have the opportunity, my most authentic source is travel experience, which puts me out in the world and interacting with people in their own cultural environment.

Do you carry a sketchbook with you?

I purchase a travel diary the instant I get to a new destination, at artisan markets or local travel shops. In Peru, I carried a small diary with me in a plastic bag to keep it dry in the Amazon rainforest. The natural colors of birds and jungle life, the local crafts, and jewelry were an intense visual experience, and I had my diary to save my thoughts, ideas, and embellishment designs as they came to me.

What do you consider when choosing a sketchbook?

A small, messenger bag–sized book is perfect for me. I can take it anywhere and the page is still large enough to work on without compromising the sketches. Sometimes with smaller books, it's difficult to sketch comfortably. I prefer wire binding because it allows my pages to lay flat.

2-45

2-45 Scott Nylund—Amazon inspiration wall.

2-46 Achoté Red Zo É beaded gown for professional presentation, rendered in color pencil with fine-tip marker outline.

2-46

2-47

RENALDO BARNETTE

Fashion designer/illustrator Renaldo Barnette grew up traveling the world, beginning his successful career at FIDM (Fashion Institute of Design and Merchandising) in Los Angeles and Parsons School of Design. Sketching and modeling in Paris after graduation, he soon became assistant designer to Patrick Kelly and later in New York City designed for Anne Klein, Nicole Miller, and Tuleh. For five years Barnette was design director for Yansi Fugel and, in 2004, launched his own women's ready-to-wear line to rave reviews. He currently designs or illustrates freelance for such designers as Polo Ralph Lauren and Tommy Hilfiger. For the last fifteen years, he has taught fashion design art at FIT.

Is a sketchbook part of your design process on the job?

Whether I'm designing luxury eveningwear or sportswear separates for the career woman, my working croquis book *is* my design process. It's filled with really rough sketches, mostly designed sitting around the table in meetings, as we're choosing fabrics and deciding on direction for the customer that season. I'm designing and merchandising at the same time as I sketch. I translate or refine these into working sketches for production as the line or collection comes together.

How do you stay inspired?

I keep a personal journal or diary—a hodgepodge of different things, from sportswear to eveningwear. I'm always thinking design, even in my quick idea sketches, writing notes about the fabrics for each piece. This book is a constant source of inspiration for me and includes images that reference my love of twentieth-century fashion and the great Donyale Luna, the first black woman to appear on any *Vogue*—my "American World Girl" muse. I always take my sketchbook with me to museum exhibits. Looking at historical fashion gives you your own reference and inspires your own sketches. If I'm ever stuck creatively, that's where I go.

Renaldo Barnette's many sketchbooks constitute a personal history of his design creativity—each one fresh and right for that time in fashion. He conducts professional fashion design drawing workshops in New York City and plans to launch an original fashion comic in the near future.

See more of his work in *Chapter 5* and online sketch demonstration at www.bloomsbury.com/rothman -fashion-sketchbook

2-48 Renaldo Barnette—professional portfolio presentation sketches freshly rendered in marker with callouts and fabric/mood page.

2-48

Would you tell me, please, which way I ought to go from here?"
"That depends a good deal on where you want to get to. 🙶🙶
—*Lewis Carroll,* Alice's Adventures in Wonderland

CHAPTER 3

MARKET RESEARCH: YOUR DESIGN DIRECTION

From multi-billion-dollar luxury brand innovators to mass-market design teams, research is how the design process begins. Market research lays the solid groundwork for building and focusing your creative ideas into a collection. And when combined with your inspirational research and individual design concept, it tells you "where you want to get to"—your design direction.

Your sketchbook research communicates your creative vision, sets you apart from your design competitors, and helps you formulate your design identity. Most designers who use sketchbooks keep a separate book for each project or collection they commit to—academic projects, competition briefs, or client design assignments. Their research and initial ideas keep them clearly focused on the necessary design objectives and parameters provided for them. But for your personal collection or job search portfolio, you are the one who provides your design objectives and sets your own parameters. By directing your creativity to the specific market level and area of design you want to work in, you will create a collection based on real market fundamentals and organized more clearly toward production.

MENSWEAR
INFLUENCES
tailoring!!!
boxy silh.
lots of buttons
pic & pad stitch
pick stitch
button ups!

3-1

3-1 Cecily Moore defines her collection theme, customer, market, and design direction in one glance . . . it's all research.

The aim of your inspiration sketchbook explorations has been to help clarify your individual aesthetic and discover concept and theme. Conducting market research, gathering in visual inspiration, and searching out sources are equally vital pre-design preparations for making the crucial choices necessary for successful design. In your role as an intern or entry-level design assistant, you will be taking on and supporting various aspects of design room research and organization. For your own project, delving into the retail market will identify your target customer from a different perspective and help you understand the business environment you will be competing in. Your sketchbook lets you think things through visually as you compare, analyze, and record your creative investigations, target your competitors, and merge your design vision into a comprehensive, reality-based design direction.

My job as designer is to enhance the personality of the brand and make it stronger.
—*Wendy Friedman, Design Director, Men's RTW: Coldweather & Sweaters, Coach, Inc.*

Design Philosophy

The philosophy that identifies your aesthetic underlies everything you do. Translated into the realm of design, it describes the key fashion messages you hold for your work and becomes your predominant stylistic expression and brand personality. Your design philosophy evolves with experience, establishing the foundation for your creativity even though your market level or brand identity may change.

3-2 Anya Zelinska's design philosophy: "Simple, easy-to-wear clothes for a strong, determined woman . . . Sexy is not what's on the surface."

For example, in designing for Celine, Phoebe Philo contributes her own "sense of street culture . . . and practicality" to the androgynous essence of the brand, making simple, fashion-forward pieces a woman will be able to wear forever. The women she designs for are modern, intelligent, unfussy, and often tomboyish: "They've got their feet on the ground." In studying her collections, we see that despite stylistic variations from season to season, her own design vision remains constant, merging with the personality of the Celine brand, ensuring a loyal following.

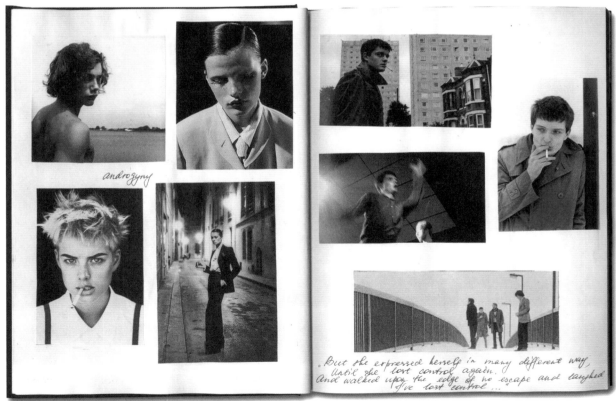

androgyny

„But she expressed herself in many different way, until she lost control again. And walked upon the edge of no escape and laughed I've lost control …

3-2

EXERCISE 5: Visualizing Your Design Philosophy

At all market levels, fashion is an aesthetics business. Satisfying emotional needs and desires creates loyal customers as much as does providing fit and quality. What key fashion messages link your aesthetic with that of your customer?

- Search fashion blogs for design philosophy quotes from designers you admire.
- Gather images that express their key fashion messages in mood and style.
- Compare the above with your own fashion style and jot down words and phrases that might develop into a working philosophy for your own design.
- Continuing in your personal sketchbook, add images that express your philosophy.

So too with Ralph Lauren, a virtuoso at creating a world of luxury and entitlement that all his customers can identify with or aspire to. For millions of Anglophile viewers of the PBS Masterpiece Theater series *Downton Abbey,* he associates himself with upper-crust lifestyle and standards of quality, evoking his design vision in brand image promotional philosophy.

Classic, to me, is something that is timeless, enduring, the things that never go out of style. The kinds of clothes I design are the kinds of things I believe in, the kinds of things that last forever.
—*Ralph Lauren*

Identifying Your Customer

It is the rare woman who can afford made-to-measure clothing today, but any woman can find virtual gratification off the peg with a label or designer who truly understands her. Your customer represents real women or men of different ages, lifestyles, and body types who share your fashion aesthetic and aspire to your fashion style in expressing their self-image.

Does that make your customer a conservative or a classic dresser? Are clean lines and simple shapes her preference, or would you classify her fashion taste as avant-garde, romantic, or edgy? Which design labels will she wear and which will she never wear? Answering these questions will help you identify your fashion style and your range of customer. The young, affluent, urban "Gossip Girl" can share the same label enthusiasm as the suburban country club matron and be miles apart in lifestyle and interests. But they come together as customers for the label's cut and fashion aesthetic, designed purposely to enhance the curvy proportions and flirty fashion style they have in common.

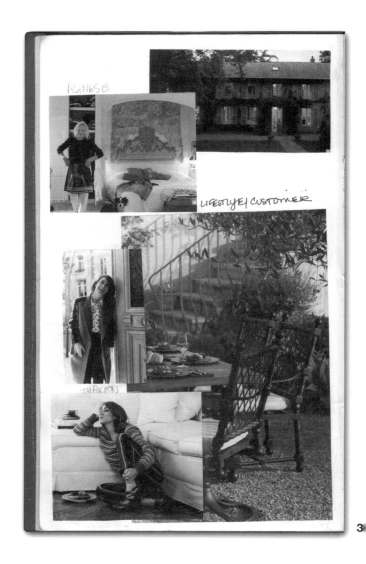

3-3 Amelia Tkach creates a visual lifestyle scenario, capturing a Mediterranean vibe to guide collection design for her culturally curious, contemporary customer.

To win her loyalty, you must discover her taste in dressing and care about her aspirations and what she loves to do. Her typical career, lifestyle, and budget will tell you how to meet her clothing needs at her financial level. To understand your customer better:

- Clip and crop images of directional silhouettes and detailing that identify your customer's fashion style.
- Make notes in your sketchbook as you imagine different lifestyle scenarios; collect images of your customer's wardrobe necessities.

To understand your customer financially, visit where she shops. Is she upmarket and shopping in luxury flagship stores and online, at Bergdorf Goodman and Net-a-Porter? Is she mid-level and shopping at Barney's and Shopbop, or is she downmarket with the masses at Zara and H&M? Consider why she wants to buy your clothes, when and how she will wear them, and how she builds her wardrobe.

Does she dress for success as a top litigator in classic Armani, or is she the price-conscious cool girl who buys hi-low and will invest in one avant-garde statement piece from Comme des Garçons each season to mix with her J. Crew basics?

3-4 For her spring/summer collection, Jessica deVries clips a mix of looks, ideas, and color inspired by her young contemporary customer's off-kilter lifestyle.

3-4

CREATIVE • WHIMSICAL • MYSTERIOUS

CUSTOMER

LOVES to
VISIT LONDON,
STOCKHOLM +
Copenhagen

CREATURES OF
THE WIND
+
ACNE
+
OPENING CEREMONY

LIVES iN the
EAST Village

ROSie

Freelance
Graphic Designer

Feminine design,
luxurious Materials,
Sultry silhouettes.
demi

3-5 Korina Brewer's hi-low customer (above): cool and creative, an independent traveler with an eclectic sense of style. Luxury meets sassy femininity (center) in Demi Chang's entitled club girl with disposable income. Ashley Gonzalez's contemporary urban customer (below) "wears classic pieces with bohemian nonchalance."

New York nonchalant streetwear chic.

The customer is a 20-30 young professional. She is highly interested in fashion and enjoys being able to afford it. She plays with tailored silhouettes along with looser fits both at home and at work.
She is simple, classic, yet sometimes a bit daring... not afraid to experiment with fashion.

3-5

A Typical Friday...

7am - Starts morning: freshly roasted coffee / skimming 'the magazine'
8am – Heads to the office in her red Manolo Blahniks and Gucci
9am – Checks her inbox and preps presentation for editorial meeting
11am – Looks up NYFW schedules and gallery openings
1pm – Lunches on salmon salad and yogurt
2pm – Press open day; checking out up-and-coming designers...
4pm – Confirms flight reservations for next month: Four Seasons in Maui
7pm – Manicure/pedicure at her favorite nail spa
9pm – Catching up with friends over champagne

3-6 Through day-planner and image choices, Gayoung Ahn shows she understands the chic, day-to-evening lifestyle of her fashion-forward career customer.

3-6

EXERCISE 6: Your Key Fashion Message

You will be combining images of customer and mood to communicate your design vision in your sketchbook. To prepare, sort through your pictures and edit them to reflect the different ages, types, and lifestyles of your customer.

- Avoid images that show another designer's brand ads or runway shots.
- Choose images that suggest your design vision and depict season and style direction. (If you intend a strong military silhouette for autumn, don't pick images of your customer dressed in soft, summery frocks.)
- Do choose headshots or cropped sportswear shots that focus on your customer's personality, mood, and aesthetic.
- Organize your images together loosely, reflect on your customer's tastes and lifestyle, and describe her in words and phrases.

Targeting Your Market

The fashion industry is broadly classified into levels of commerce that establish price point and the quality of materials and craftsmanship it affords. These market classifications make design planning possible and facilitate the business of clothing production and sales. Designers set themselves apart from their competitors within each segment through individual aesthetic, design style, and customer affinity. Therefore, understanding current market forces, knowing where you stand in the market and who you are in competition with, is vital to your success.

Each region of fashion's global marketplace understands and references the various levels in similar terms, with the European and American sportswear classifications leading the conversation. Fashion has traditionally started with the masters of haute couture, becoming more accessible and less exclusive off the peg with each successive downmarket level.

3-7 Gayoung Ahn targets her upmarket positioning in-store. She finds further research in magazines and online, which inspire design ideas for her collection. (See Gayoung's final edit sketches in Chapter 5.)

3-7

As a designer, you must love your customer . . . know what she needs for her life and romance her.
—*Mark Waldrop, VP Design Collections, Jones Apparel Group*

[handwritten annotations on photos:]
← extremely love Hair + face + MOOD!
← love, love Size + Volu of swe
← love pencil sk
FAVORITE EDITORIAL SHOT OF THE SEAS

LOVING THE "SLOUCH"
IN LOVE WITH HER →
HATS PULLED WAY DOWN!
GREAT HAT + HAIR ←

3-8 Beloved guest critic and inspiring designer Mark Waldrop (1965–2012) shared research while briefing students for FIT Fashion Design Critic's Award Project, fall 2009. He found inspiration for contemporary customer styling and mood in an upmarket editorial shot and Christopher Bailey's Burberry Prorsum runway.

3-8

E-commerce and the recent economic rewind have brought greater price fluidity across traditional market segments and allowed brand presence to reach all levels of society at once. Many design brands have several lines, each targeted to a different market level, and often venture into collaborations with mass-market retail chains.

Even young independent labels find that such partnerships broaden their customer base without diluting their brand. Today's upscale woman might shop Target's designer capsule collections, while her mainstream counterpart will find the right dress for a special event from a contemporary label online.

Retail Observations

Department stores know their customer well and hire teams to track her preferences and buying habits. They buy and position merchandise on the selling floor according to price point and style. This makes it easier for the shopper to find what she likes and needs—and for you to find your design niche and customer. Your design competitors will share the same market segment, price point, and area of specialization and have a similar stylistic approach to design.

For example, in Saks Fifth Avenue or Nordstrom, you might find the clean-lined, upmarket simplicity of Celine positioned next to Calvin Klein.

By contrast, in a designer's flagship store or boutique, you will likely find the full season's collection. The shop's design and décor have been carefully chosen to idealize brand image and attract its ideal clientele.

Design decisions are based on understanding market and brand identity, design philosophy, and customer—your own and your target designers'. Start by evaluating how competitors in your same market level attract a solid customer base. In comparing the pieces they offer and determining their best-selling styles, you will have a better idea of the looks you might want to develop for your collection.

La Perla @ Saks fifth Avenue

Silk Satin Demi Bra
- Underwire cups with contrast floral lace.
- Silk
- $ 298.00

Silk Satin Thong
- Floral lace at hip.
- Silk
- $ 175.00

Lace Bodysuit
- Underwire cups with floral lace.
- Sheer striped mesh bodice with black center panel.
- Floral lace at hips.
- Nylon
- $ 394.00

Lace Thong
- Floral lace at front
- Cotton/Spandex
- $62.00

3-9 Miki Kawaguchi's market research includes exquisite Intimate flats, retail price, fabric, and detailing information.

3-9

Two Essential Steps in Market Research

First, visit an upmarket department store and shop the floors with sketchbook in hand. Observe various market levels as differentiated by price and style. Find the designers who share your aesthetic and attract the customer you want to design for. Learn all you can by studying their collections and reading price tags and labels. Then visit their flagship stores, or freestanding boutiques, and compare the same information you learned on the department store floor.

Your second essential step is to analyze your aspirational designers' online collections, tracking them back through several consecutive seasons. Compare the seasonal evolution of silhouette, range of looks, color, and fabric. Investigate their public image and design philosophy in trade publications, official web sites and print advertising, and online fashion blog presence.

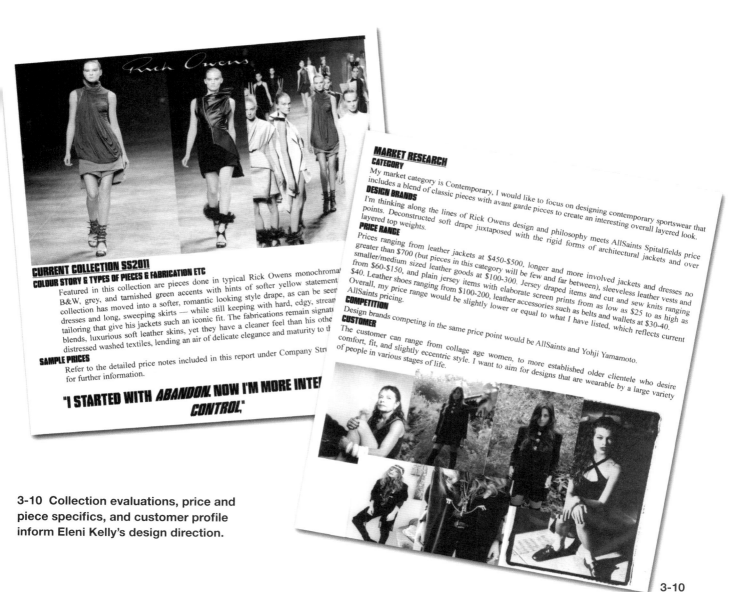

CURRENT COLLECTION SS2011
COLOUR STORY & TYPES OF PIECES & FABRICATION ETC

Featured in this collection are pieces done in typical Rick Owens monochroma[t] B&W, grey, and tarnished green accents with hints of softer yellow statement collection has moved into a softer, romantic looking style drape, as can be seen dresses and long, sweeping skirts — while still keeping with hard, edgy, strea[m] tailoring that give his jackets such an iconic fit. The fabrications remain signat[u] blends, luxurious soft leather skins, yet they have a cleaner feel than his oth[e] distressed washed textiles, lending an air of delicate elegance and maturity to t[h]

SAMPLE PRICES

Refer to the detailed price notes included in this report under Company Str[u] for further information.

"I STARTED WITH *ABANDON*. NOW I'M MORE INTE[N] *CONTROL.*"

MARKET RESEARCH
CATEGORY

My market category is Contemporary, I would like to focus on designing contemporary sportswear that includes a blend of classic pieces with avant garde pieces to create an interesting overall layered look.

DESIGN BRANDS

I'm thinking along the lines of Rick Owens design and philosophy meets AllSaints Spitalfields price points. Deconstructed soft drape juxtaposed with the rigid forms of architectural jackets and over layered top weights.

PRICE RANGE

Prices ranging from leather jackets at $450-$500, longer and more involved jackets and dresses no greater than $700 (but pieces in this category will be few and far between), sleeveless leather vests and smaller/medium sized leather goods at $100-300. Jersey draped items and cut and sew knits ranging from $60-$150, and plain jersey items with elaborate screen prints from as low as $25 to as high as $40. Leather shoes ranging from $100-200, leather accessories such as belts and wallets at $30-40. Overall, my price range would be slightly lower or equal to what I have listed, which reflects current AllSaints pricing.

COMPETITION

Design brands competing in the same price point would be AllSaints and Yohji Yamamoto.

CUSTOMER

The customer can range from collage age women, to more established older clientele who desire comfort, fit, and slightly eccentric style. I want to aim for designs that are wearable by a large variety of people in various stages of life.

3-10 Collection evaluations, price and piece specifics, and customer profile inform Eleni Kelly's design direction.

3-10

EXERCISE 7: Market and Customer Analysis

In-Store/In-Person

Which market level appeals to your design aspirations?
- Compare upmarket collections with those selling for less.
- Determine your market level and area of concentration.

Where would you position your collection?
- Find two adjacent designers who share your design aesthetic.
- How is their design style similar; what sets them apart?
- What connects your design style and aesthetic to theirs?

Designer comparison and analysis
- Analyze both collections in-store; compare silhouette, color, fabric, and detail.
- Determine price point for both by checking the range of key garment prices: coat, jacket, dress, skirt, pant, and top.
- Note the range of pieces offered in both collections; identify key pieces.
- Sketch directional styles and details, using callouts; snap photo details.

Online—Public image and promotional
- Gather visuals of customer, logo, and brand image for both designers.
- Note the design style and aesthetic they present.

Online/Look book—Timeline analysis of past collections and seasons
- Compare the collections, then and now; identify key silhouettes.
- Briefly analyze the evolution of key silhouettes, color, and detail for both.
- What pieces do they include? Consistent silhouettes and pieces indicate best-selling looks. Note the range and concentration of pieces.
- Print out and identify directional looks by season, year, and designer.

Organizing Your Research

In such a research-heavy field as fashion design, the ordering of images, sketches, information, and materials is indispensable for any design team. Corporate design labels have separate research and concept teams that provide direction for the seasonal collections. Nevertheless, individual designers will do their own personal research and find their best method of organizing it for easy access and communication of ideas.

Most employ a combination of image bank archiving and desktop folders, using both smart devices and computers, then print out the images that grab their attention within the context of concept and theme. These go into actual folders with their magazine clippings for use in brainstorming a collection and sketching out associated directional ideas. Handling your images as you remix accelerates visual associations and design thinking. Sketchbooks are also used for archiving design direction, development sketches, and notations by season and delivery—a valuable resource for future inspiration and reminder of best-selling silhouettes.

Categorizing Your Research

Organize a system that works smoothly for you by sorting your market research and images into categories for design direction. Try these to start:

- Concept/theme/season/design philosophy/customer
- Competitor: timeline visuals/brand image and ads/company structure
- Market level and price point information

3-11 With linear patterning, Wei Lin creates a visual connection between archived fashion research and thematic agate structures.

3-11

> **Runway collection is about strength and vision and 'the message.' Commercial collection is about practicality and the streamlining of all those elements.**
> —Daniel Roseberry

Visualizing Your Design Direction

No matter how celebrated a designer's artistic vision may be, it needs the oxygen of funding for press recognition and creative acknowledgment. Commercial versions of runway collections exist for that reason, sold off the peg in exclusive designer shops and filtered downmarket into secondary lines like Valentino Red and McQ.

Great value is placed on the success of coveted luxury products, accessories, and fragrance and transition collections such as resort or pre-fall. These allow upper-echelon fashion innovation to survive. It takes considered creativity and a keen grasp of market constraints to streamline fantasy into wearable reality.

3-12 Nicole Goh targets her moderate customer as "chic, forward, and effortlessly confident." Her pre-fall delivery inspires high-tech fabrics and athletic detailing for "trend-right basics and must-have statement pieces."

3-12

Even at the conceptual stage, designs have to respect price point and make sense from a customer standpoint as well. Your research analysis gives you the information you need to take on the creative challenges of blending your design vision with commercial practicalities. Your sketchbook acts as a visual proving ground for the direction you are deciding for your collection.

How Market Defines Sketchbook Design Direction

Your sketchbook should talk your market's language in the way you visually communicate your design direction:

Designer Ready-to-Wear/Pret-a-Porter

The higher the market level, the more conceptual and inclusive of sketches your initial thinking should be, with visual metaphor evolving into directional designs.

- Think luxurious, innovative style and detailing, precious quality fabrics and embellishments, advanced print technology, and rich subtle color.

Mid-Level/Contemporary

Your directional ideas will be influenced by theme and customer aspiration, career or trend dynamics, merchandising, and sales for your design arena.

- Think upmarket adaptation, functional silhouette, mixable pieces, comfortable and high-tech fabrics, fashion-forward prints, wearable colors, and bright accents.

Mass Market/Mainstream

At downmarket price points, function, wearability, and theme are your strongest research focus; your designs must also perform as necessary wardrobe pieces.

- Think casual, practical wardrobe basics, derivative style and detail, comfortable easy-care fabrics, bright graphics, and standard, fun colors.

Read more about the effects of market on design development in *Chapter 4*.

3-13 Personal sketchbooks.

3-13

THE CABINET OF DR. CALIGARI

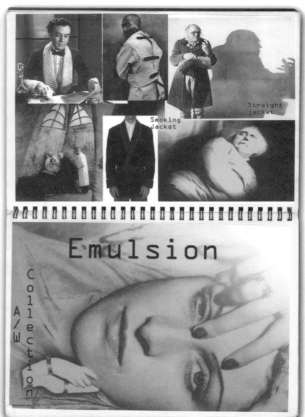

Smoking Jacket

Straight jacket

Emulsion

A/W Collection

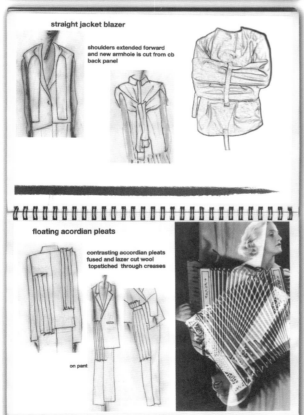

straight jacket blazer

shoulders extended forward
and new armhole is cut from cb
back panel

floating acordian pleats

contrasting accordian pleats
fused and lazer cut wool
topstiched through creases

on pant

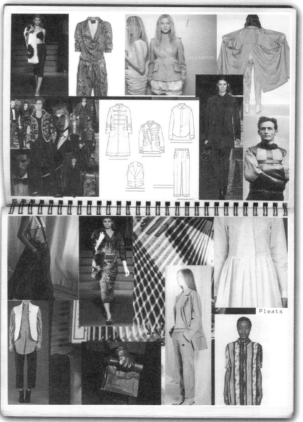

Pleats

3-14

EXERCISE 8: Visualizing Your Design Direction

Visualizing the direction you intend for your collection design involves using a combination of images, sketches, and words that allow your pre-collection ideas to gel and prepares you for developing them further.

Select and transfer your images to a working surface (tabletop, floor, pin board) for use in remixing and editing your key elements. Experiment by loosely grouping images, sketches, and references that express your concept. Your object is to link your separate design ideas within the context of your concept and theme.

Your design direction should include the following visuals:
- Core conceptual ideas and seasonal theme
- Cultural, style/trend influences that establish silhouette and detailing
- Customer/muse—her look should embody your collection style/attitude
- Directional sketches, seasonal colors, fabrics and prints to express concept and theme; callouts to define

Dedicate your sketchbook space now to this purpose, focusing your trials into one design direction. When all the pieces fall into place, you can start planning the first pages of your new process sketchbook. Approach it by creating a series of expressive pages that unify your significant research elements and mood and inspiration images into a comprehensive direction for your collection design, as in the examples you see on these pages.

But first, check out your process sketchbook options and techniques in *Chapter 4*.

3-14 Two early twentieth-century, avant-garde influences, Man Ray and Robert Weine, converge in Ethan Ianniello's conceptual narrative for designer price point collection, informed by directional sketches and current fashion research.

3-15

NAAMA DOKTOFSKY

World traveler Naama Doktofsky was born and raised in Israel and graduated summa cum laude with a BFA in fashion design from FIT. While at FIT, she received an Honorable Mention from the CFDA (Council of Fashion Designers of America) Scholarship competition and interned for Reed Krakoff and Donna Karan Collection, among others. After two years as associate designer for Yigal Azrouel's high-end sportswear collection, Naama is currently the designer for Shoshanna, RTW and Evening Collections.

What elements make a strong start to a sketchbook?

Interviewers see so many candidates' books, and putting your name on your sketchbook cover page gives them a second chance to connect your name with what they see. Your first spread should be about the essence of your collection—a first sketch shows your aesthetic, design direction, and sketching ability; add a nonfashion image or two that represent your theme and key words to guide you as you design. It's really hard to design if you don't have some sort of vision. And I think it is important to show that you get inspiration from many different aspects of life, not just fashion.

Is there a formula for a fashion design sketchbook?

This is your own sketchbook—it's your baby, so you really want it to shine. You really want to set yourself apart, but there is no formula in the way you do it. Whatever you feel most comfortable and confident in doing will translate the best for you. If you feel you are strongest at designing dresses or outerwear, maybe you need to focus on that: "This is what I'm strongest in, this is what I love"—because usually if you love it, it's going to be your best.

What role does the sketchbook play in interviewing for a job?

A sketchbook is one of the most important pieces you have going into an interview, because it shines a light on your design process, which doesn't show in the final portfolio. Here, the viewer can see how you go about designing a collection and know if you share their design view and aesthetic.

Part of your career success has been that you work from a plan . . .

I left everything behind when I came here, so to do this I felt I had to make a plan. In school I thought about what kind of designers I wanted to work for, researched them, and made a list of companies I thought would be good for me. Then I focused my whole design process toward that goal. I also got a job working in Yigal Azrouel's store and made the personal connection for my first job. I think a personal connection is just as important as your sketchbook and portfolio.

See Naama Doktofsky's work throughout this book and her video interview and sketchbook tour online at www.bloomsbury.com/rothman-fashion-sketchbook

3-16 Naama Doktofsky—portfolio presentation sketch in marker and color pencil.

3-16

3-17

DANIEL SILVERSTEIN

As a student at FIT, Daniel Silverstein interned extensively and studied abroad in Milan. When introduced to the concept of zero fabric waste in design, he was galvanized to challenge the industry paradigm of reckless waste, using his own zero-waste techniques. In 2010, after graduating summa cum laude with a BFA in fashion design at age 21, he co-launched his collection, 100% NY. After appearing as a finalist on NBC's Fashion Star, *he successfully re-launched his brand, Daniel Silverstein, in New York's garment district.*

Do you use a sketchbook in your design process?

I sketch whenever I'm inspired, and later compile them into my sketchbook. When I'm thinking creatively, I'm very mobile as I sketch. Setting up one space where you're supposed to do creative thinking feels very challenging. So I find that being able to work anywhere and bring it back to my design studio is much more helpful for me. I use a magnet board so I can move my images around easily when I'm designing.

What is your design vision or philosophy?

One of my key principles is responsibility in design. For me zero waste is a way of patternmaking, cutting, and thinking, not a price point or a look. Any designer can do this and still be competitive. The second is to design considerately of the customer. I see her as an edgy, sexy, style influencer who likes to be noticed. So I want to help her stand out from the crowd and provide pieces in each collection for her every body type and age range, for every aspect of her life.

Do you focus your intuitive design process into a theme for collection?

Definitely. I find inspiration in whatever moves me. A book of bird photographs became the inspiration for one whole collection. A line from an otherwise forgettable film inspired me to translate it into an original art print, which I incorporated into my best-selling designs for another collection—a great way to give my customer the things she loves from me, but in exciting new versions.

Daniel Silverstein's video interview and sketchbook tour are available for viewing online at www.bloomsbury.com /rothman-fashion-sketchbook

3-18

3-18 Daniel Silverstein—design studio pin board for fall 2013.

3-19 Daniel Silverstein—pewter Spine Dress, fall 2014 (right). Photographer: Maeghan Donohue

3-19

I was interning when a job opportunity opened up for the design team. My portfolio was a good fit, but they wanted to see how I arrived at my finished designs. It was my sketchbook that got me the job.

—*Ryan Ocampo, designer, Michael Kors*

CHAPTER 4

DESIGN DEVELOPMENT: THE PROCESS SKETCHBOOK

The pages of your process sketchbook are a working progression of trial and error—not a project in itself. Developing your designs in a sketchbook helps to actualize your creative thinking. It is a visually triggered process, layering your sketches and associated ideas, in tune with your original intentions and the customer you are designing for. You are not merely archiving what you have done but are actively engaged in creating a living document of how you arrived at your collection.

Your process sketchbook showcases your design thinking in the rough and is ideal for defining yourself as a designer. Thanks to its dual role as open studio space and personal design lab, you learn to think and work sequentially within a specific market, sharpen your strengths, and discover how to design through or around your creative blocks. It offers the opportunity to learn what you may want to change and how best to showcase your greatest assets as a designer (*Chapter 5*). By evaluating how others have approached their design process, you may discover ways to minimize your challenges and support your individual voice.

4-1

4-1 Amanda Robertson formats her sketchbook like a flip chart, infusing her pages with color and vitality.

4-2 Amanda's key research elements instantly communicate her design direction for fall/winter collection development. Her informal layouts are in sync with her culturally aware, contemporary fashion message—simple, clear, bold, energetic.

4-2

> I *always* keep a sketchbook with me. I have a cupboard full of them—one for each collection I've designed over the years. They are an amazing resource for me.
>
> —Yolande Heijnen, VP Design Director, Joe Fresh

Sketchbook Options

Dedicate a new sketchbook for developing your design process. Its purpose is for working, so choose one that is functional and worthy of your collection, with room enough for your design experiments. To keep it portable, consider sketchbook sizes ranging between 8" × 10" and 9" × 12". If you like working large, 11" × 14" is for you, although it can be a bit cumbersome or heavy for some. In deciding on book format, think about what works best for you:

- horizontal (landscape) format, with enough page width to sketch out a line of thumbnail croquis
- vertical (portrait) format, with ample room to play around on the page

Both can read left to right, as in most books, or bottom to top, like a flip chart.

4-3 Eleni Kelly's horizontal landscape book format provides space for her well-merchandised summary of looks, organized into itemized groupings for Fall II delivery and ready for final color edit.

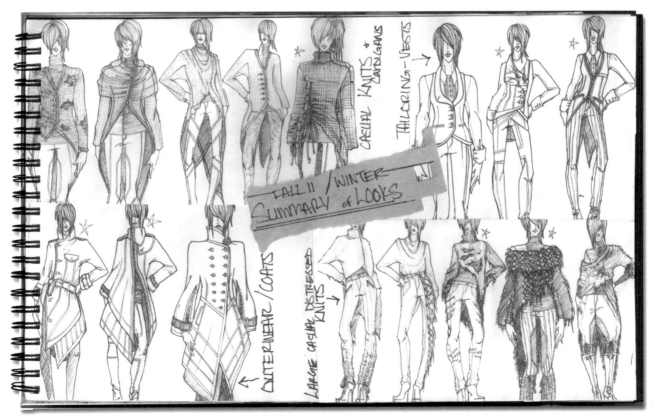

4-3

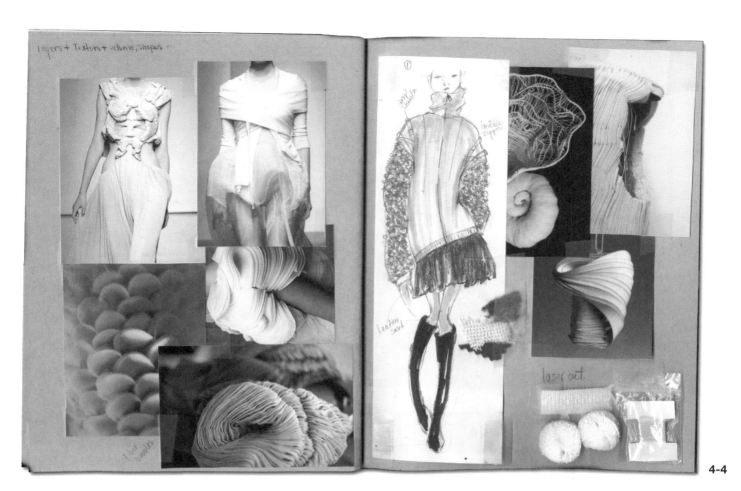

4-4 Making good use of the vertical format, Andreina Jiminez shows her conceptual direction by combining the original source images and fashion photos that inspired her development sketch.

Ease of use is your primary concern, so make sure that the pages are securely bound and that the binding is sturdy and allows all the pages to lie flat when open. Check that the paper is archival and will accept marker or watercolor without bleeding through or buckling (minimum paper weight: 65#). You already know what you like about your inspiration/research sketchbook and what features don't work for you.

Besides letting your experience influence your new sketchbook purchase, you also want to consider in advance your easiest way of working: is it directly on your pages, or are you more comfortable working outside your book, then cutting and pasting in later? Think about how you like to arrange elements on your sketchbook pages—do you use the whole available space or only part of it? Does it bother you when visuals are not balanced on a page? Or perhaps you like a bit of imperfection?

Sketchbook Criteria

Designing begins with experimentation and making connections. So before you begin processing your design ideas through the practicalities of fit and product, first allow them to emerge and take on a life of their own, just as you did in your personal sketchbook diary. Invention comes from following wherever those ideas may lead you. However you do it, the way you work it out for yourself in your sketchbook becomes your design story—a visual telling of your internal creative process. There is no formula for doing this, but you have the benefit of time-tested criteria to help you unify and focus your ideas as you design. I will be suggesting a sketchbook progression that allows you the freedom to discover your own best methods of working. Later, as you organize and edit your ideas into a cohesive collection, you will see where you need to make adjustments and re-work designs. You will discover whether you have given yourself clear enough guidelines to move forward easily, or if you need to go back and include additional elements from your research.

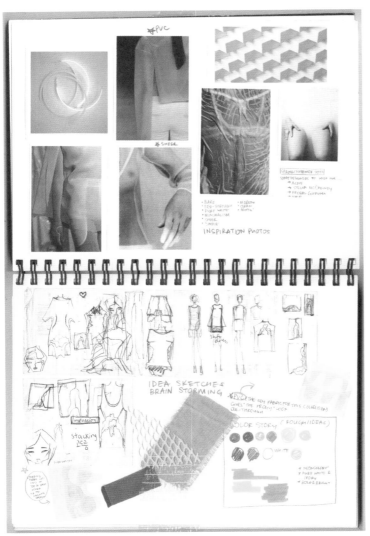

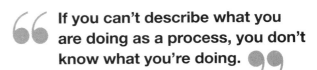

If you can't describe what you are doing as a process, you don't know what you're doing.
—*W. Edwards Deming*

4-5 Sooyeon Bang experiments with her sketchbook design direction in a consistent flip-chart format.

4-5

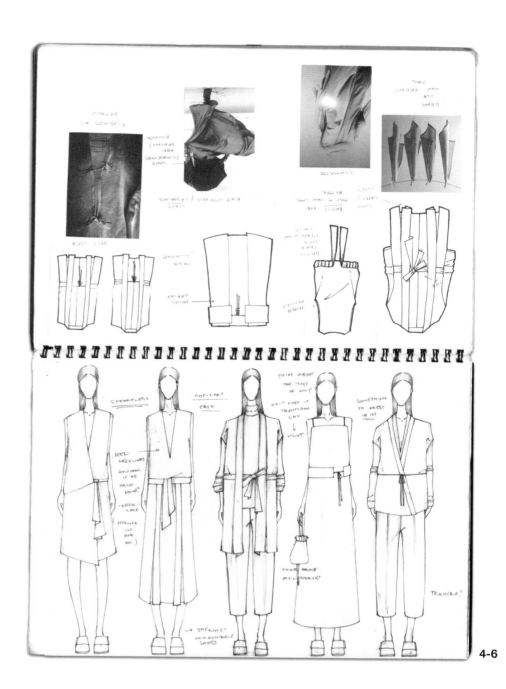

> **"** In a consistent book format, each page carries the eye to the next, with no blank pages to stop the advance. **"**

4-6 Jose Camacho's lapse in consistent book format creates a disconnect between his cohesively developed design sketches and the associated images and flats that would have placed them in context.

4-6

Consistent Book Format

A consistent book format allows you to push the limits of your creativity and still send the essential visual message that you are focused in your thinking and understand the natural progression of design. In a consistent book format, each page carries the eye to the next, with no blank pages to stop the advance. If you begin by working horizontally on your pages, you should continue working horizontally throughout your entire book. Switching your content to vertical midstream interrupts the attention of your viewer and is a major inhibitor of the visual flow inherent in your process.

Sequential Progression

Your ability to think design in a logical sequence will help evolve your conceptual story so that all the elements make collective sense. Even if your actual design process doesn't flow in an orderly progression, your book sequence should advance your collection visually, from start to finish. Your process first needs to show who you are, what inspires you, and how your research and customer shape your direction. As conceptual ideas begin to gel on your pages, combine them with your initial sketches, mood, color, and fabric. You can see if they come together well or miss the mark, so you can judge which ideas to develop further. This progression can be enormously helpful in keeping you on track and moving forward to the visual edition of your final cut.

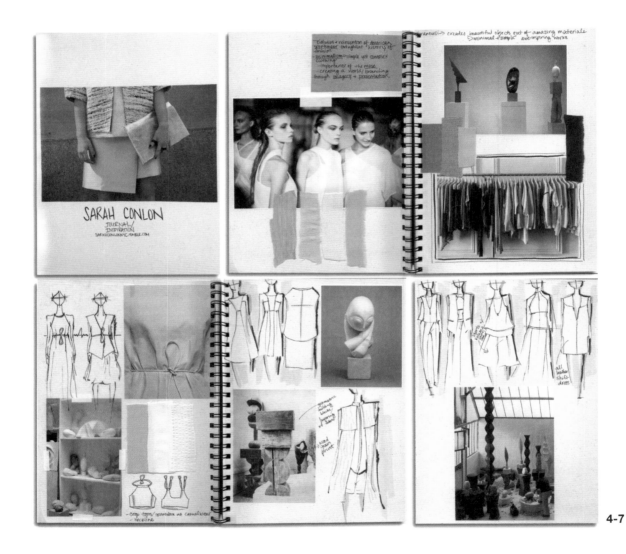

4-7

4-7 and 4-8 Working from a clear design plan for her presentation sketchbook, Sarah Conlon creates a strong, unified brand image in sequential progression, from title page through a series of commanding layout variations that link conceptual motif to design with unwavering aesthetic.

See Sarah's full sketchbook video tour online at www.bloomsbury.com/rothman-fashion-sketchbook

Essential Content for Process Sketchbook

Overview
- Cover page—identity, aesthetic, taste level
- Design philosophy/vision—brief and concise
- Customer range

Design direction—per collection or delivery
- Title—season and theme
- Original source research—inspirational non-fashion images
- Secondary research—influential fashion images
- Directional explorations—sketches and fabrics
- Design plan, merchandising notations, callouts

Concept to design process—per collection
- Color inspiration and palette
- Fabric story in varying weights and relationships
- Design development sketches, process draping
- Initial editing process, partial
- Final collection edit, sequential flow of color and fabric
- Hand-sketched flats, pop-ups of key design details
- Hand techniques, fabric manipulations; construction/pattern inventions
- Styling—sketches exploring muse, hair, makeup, accessories

See *Exercise 7* for general merchandising variables according to market.

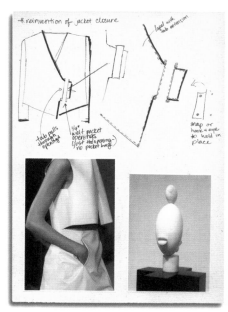
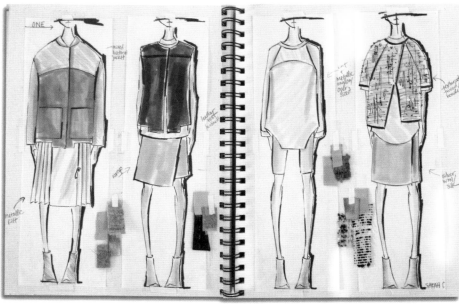

4-8

Design Direction to Plan of Action

As you begin development in earnest, take the time to formulate a design plan and set your creative goals. These can and do change as you design, but if your plan is based on smart collection strategies and merchandising decisions for customer and market, it acts as a design checklist and essential editing tool. For a project or competition, your brief more closely dictates your plan of action.

Although much smaller in size and scale, your final cut should suggest a similar proportion of looks as the runway collections in your comparative market analysis. To guide you in making key merchandising choices, compare the balance and rhythm of pieces in the line-ups you studied. Observe smart editing strategies, such as repeating color, fabric, and silhouette to create mini-groupings within the overall flow of a full collection. These kinds of design plan choices accommodate specific retail demographics and customer preferences. Look for a close run of a single look, presented in varying lengths and intensity of detail; analyze core silhouettes adapted across the seasons.

 It's the designer's responsibility to know with every certainty that the collection will make sense, it will be complete, and on time.
—*Daniel Silverstein*

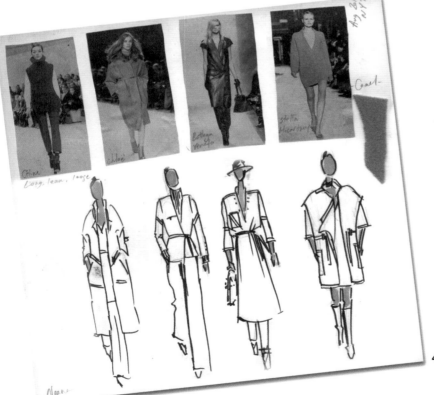

4-9 Rather than designing unrelated pieces, Naama Doktofsky begins her collection development by creating a balanced mini-grouping of core pieces, styling the total look and attitude with her first design ideas.

4-9

Design Plan Guidelines—Women's Sportswear Portfolio

Luxury/Designer Ready-to-Wear

- Showcase a minimum of two seasonal collections, fall/winter and spring/summer, with an optional small transition group bridging the two, for example, holiday, resort, or pre-fall.
- Fifteen to twenty looks can represent one day-to-evening collection; the optional transition group of seven looks may instead focus on a design interest, for example, knitwear.
- Core pieces: outerwear, jackets, woven and knit tops, pants, skirts, and dresses, which vary with season and customer; augmented by a few statement looks, such as dramatic fur, extreme silhouette, or gala evening.

Contemporary/Mid-Level

- Develop your collection as two deliveries for each of the two major seasons, fall/winter and spring/summer, with a third group as a transition between the two, for example, holiday, resort, or pre-fall.
- Seven to ten looks comprise each season delivery; a transition group (seven looks) can be more flats-oriented and focused on merchandising (e.g., look book).
- Core pieces: coordinated outerwear, jackets, woven and knit tops, pants, skirts, and dresses, which vary with season, customer, and area of concentration, such as denim. Best-sellers are adapted across the seasons to reflect changing trends, and looks are merchandised in groups by mixing core and standout trend pieces.

4-10 Rebecca Homen organizes her key directional information at a glance on three focused, organically expressed sketchbook spreads, deftly combining mood, concept, and theme visuals with merchandising direction, and fabric story. Rebecca's design direction menu clearly defines her design philosophy and keeps her on track in collection development.

4-10

> **Design is not just what it looks like and feels like. Design is how it works.**
> —*Steve Jobs*

EXERCISE 9: Your Design Plan

1. As outlined above, revisit your market research and collection observations and comparisons and base your design plan decisions on
   - seasonal delivery calendar
   - collection strategies
   - merchandising considerations

2. Expand on your design direction (*Chapter 3, Exercise 8*) by adding practical guidelines that reflect the merchandising realities of your target market and lifestyle needs of your customer. There is room for flexibility in merchandising your collection according to your individual combination of project variables: your customer, season, area of design concentration, and design philosophy.

3. List your projected core pieces in your sketchbook. This simple bit of planning can be a great benefit in focusing your development process for collection. It will keep you on course as you create your cohesive groupings.

4. Jot down key design plan notations and callouts to explain your design ideas and connect them with your relevant research visuals and merchandising strategies.

Translating Concept into Design

The power of visual metaphor is the key to sketchbook communication. By showing the associations your mind makes between inspiring images and your design ideas, you create a visual link that is instantly understood. It explains your creative process for you as you design. If your connections are not clear to you, your process will be unclear on the sketchbook page. By themselves, your concept images don't convey your thoughts and the associations you are making or explain their influence on your design thinking.

You create meaning when you juxtapose your fabrics and design sketches with the images that inspired them. Word menus or callouts explain in words what might get lost in visual translation.

> 66 The power of visual metaphor is the key to sketchbook communication. 99

4-11 Feride Ozsoy makes a clear visual link showing her creative translation of concept into design, although the scale and placement of images dominate her delicate sketches.

4-12 Young Joon Oh's exceptional creative thinking translates visual metaphor into original design, interpreting his concept of insect-as-jacket, without getting literal. He envisions the insect exoskeleton as a stiff exterior fabric in his experimental design sketches and translates deconstructed insect parts as silhouette and seaming for an innovative final design.

4-11

4-12

4-13 Anna Hart Turner (top) translates concept into design with a sense of visual whimsy. Carter Kidd's cool visual connections with 2D geometric shapes (center) prompt new ideas for placement and proportion of detail. Daniel Silverstein's creative strength (below) lies in designing from visual metaphor in variations of scale and function.

4-13

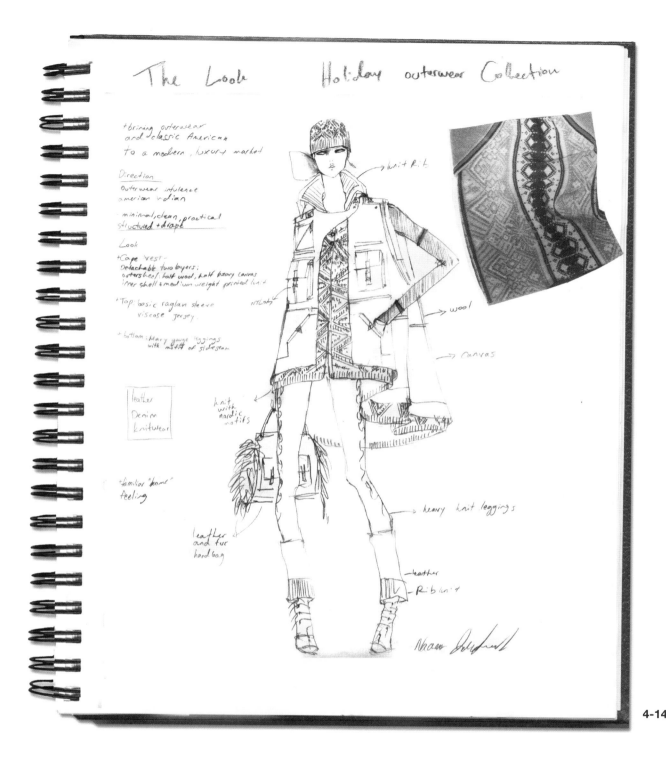

4-14

4-14 Naama Doktofsky introduces her holiday outerwear collection in her sketchbook with one defining look, styled with attitude and sketched with expert technical understanding. Her conceptual direction says she's thinking the business of design as she creates. The Nordic pattern is a central design motif, and directional notations set the stage for further development.

See the full tour of Naama's sketchbook at www.bloomsbury.com/rothman-fashion-sketchbook

Conveying Theme in Color and Fabric

The fabric you choose for your collection should embody your concept in drape, texture, pattern, volume, color, and value. A fabric story has a strong thread of color that runs through it, connecting texture and weight with values of light and shade. It balances a collection on many levels. Using visual metaphor helps you tell your color and fabric story by juxtaposing color harmony, texture, and pattern similarities with the emotional mood found in your theme images. Our response to color is usually immediate and instinctive, conjuring up seasonal and emotional connections, so it easily conveys conceptual meaning.

A varied, concept-inspired color palette pulls your fabrics together in context and brings richness and emotional resonance to your designs. Both color and fabric are instant barometers for taste level. The higher and more refined your awareness, the more subtle and sensitive to quality and detail your choices will be.

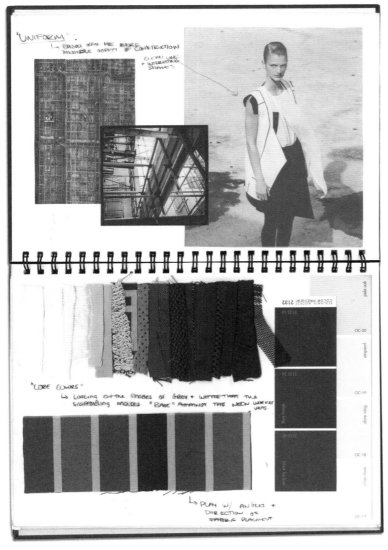

4-15 Matthew Harwoodstone's fabric story moves in a logical flow of merchandised basics, white to gray to black, in a varied textural palette. The use of visual touchstones and callouts unite his double-page layout and make his thinking instantly understandable.

> **I put together my color and fabric before I start designing. Feeling the fabric helps me think about how I'll be using it, and if I'll be able to construct the garments I have in mind.**
> —*Matthew Harwoodstone*

4-15

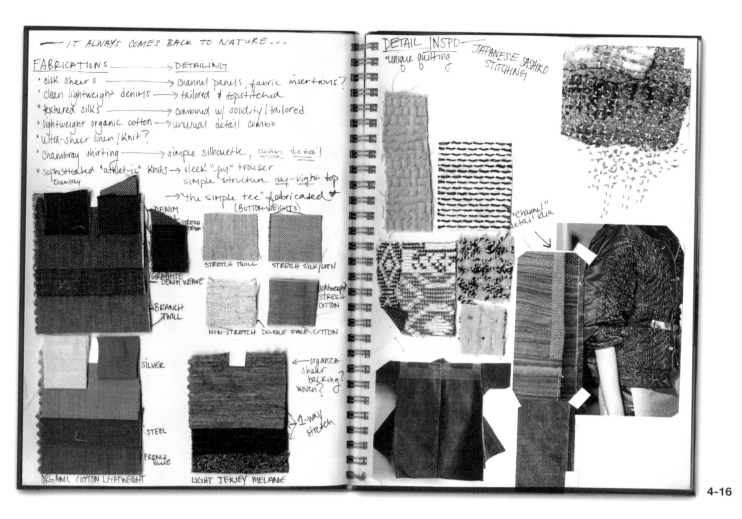

4-16 Rebecca Homen's fabric pages are rich in design and merchandising direction. Her fabric choices convey the color and textural message of her "back to nature" theme, bolstered by unique quilting and sashiko stitching detail, for a great example of how to convey design concept through fabric.

Building a Fabric Story

Depending on demographics and delivery, a collection should reflect the changing seasons, from crisp autumn days to frigid winter, or from spring showers to summer heat. Select the highest-quality fabrics available within your price point in a variety of seasonable weights, weaves, knits, textures, patterns, and prints that serve the function of each garment. A cohesive base of colors and fabrics is necessary at all market levels to anchor your design story in collection and balance the intensity of your accent fabrics. Show that you have new ideas to offer by including interesting fabric compositions, manipulations, an original knit stitch, or a print extracted from your theme images.

4-17

4-17 For her collection theme, Julie Rose Romano identifies with Mary Lennox, the heroine of a favorite childhood storybook, *The Secret Garden*, by Frances Hodgson Burnett.

" Mary summed up the loss and isolation I felt after my father's death, the emotions at the heart of my fall/winter collection. These feelings translated into seeking emotional warmth through the physical warmth of cozy wool coatings and thick knits—the 'Mary' fabrics of my collection. Another main character, Dickon, inspired colors and fabrics with a homespun, English countryside feeling—soft, woolen plaid and herringbone tweed fabrics felt safe and nurturing. "

—*Julie Rose Romano*

EXERCISE 10: Conveying Theme in Color and Fabric

Consider how color and fabric qualities convey mood and metaphor:
- Color—Variations in intensity and value: red, orange, and yellow attract, advance, and gather; blue, green, and purple calm, cool, and relax; white and pales codify cleanliness and purity; black exemplifies strength and savvy; neutrals stabilize and nurture; high-intensity colors pop; dark colors recede
- Fabric hand and surface appeal—Soft, stiff, stretchable, nubby, slick, sheer, dense, spongy, smooth, coarse, dry, crisp, shiny
- Emotional response—Touchable, dependable, delicate, comfortable, cozy, airy, precious, familiar, revealing, protective
- Wearability—How fabric wears, washes, and feels on the body
- Textile innovation—Technological advances, sustainable techniques

Choose a color palette from your key visuals and begin your fabric explorations:
- Know your customer's tastes and desires.
- Choose quality fabrics that create the shape and drape of your designs and define seasonal themes; describe their qualities.
- Organize them into workable groups based on your design plan or season.
- Arrange your mix of fabrics to show the flow of color, one into the other, positioning darker colors and base cloth below and pale or accent colors higher on the page for balance.
- Contrasting elements enhance each other; if fabric matches background, it will be camouflaged or disappear. Never show black fabric against a black background, nor white against white.
- Experiment in customizing fabric swatches by bleaching, over-dying, stitching, quilting, and so on.
- Create original prints from your own art or photos, public domain images, or random patterns/ textures; use software for image manipulations and variations in scale.

Design Development: The Main Event

This is my favorite part of the story, where you bring me into your process as you work it through. If I had only one message for you about sketchbook design development, it would be this: Design is a nuanced, visual language that must be spoken clearly and understood among collaborators. Your idea of proportion should be consistent, even in your roughest sketches. You will be eager to expand and evolve your designs by rearranging and remixing suggestions of motif and proportion found in your directional research. To make your collection work as one coherent unit, each garment should be valued as a necessary part of the whole.

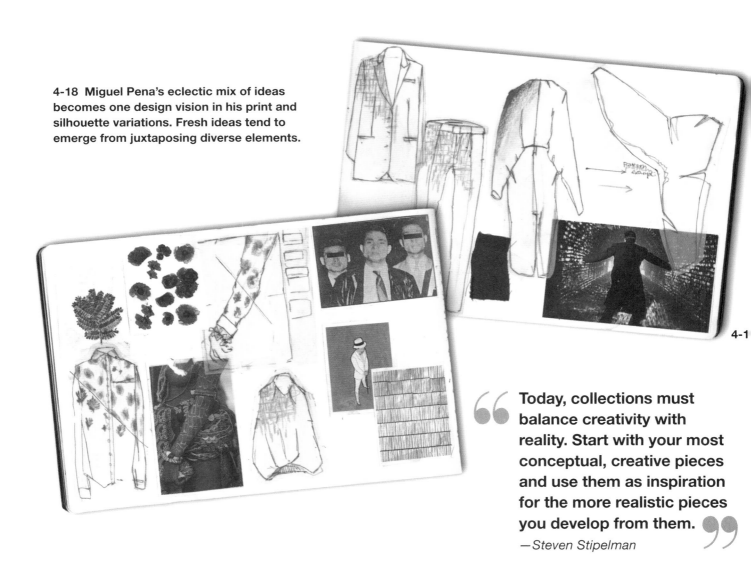

4-18 Miguel Pena's eclectic mix of ideas becomes one design vision in his print and silhouette variations. Fresh ideas tend to emerge from juxtaposing diverse elements.

4-1

> **Today, collections must balance creativity with reality. Start with your most conceptual, creative pieces and use them as inspiration for the more realistic pieces you develop from them.**
> —*Steven Stipelman*

> There are major commercial realities that should go hand in hand in the design process. If you feel that fight between the creative process and function as you design, there's something wrong.
>
> —*Daniel Roseberry*

First Steps in Development

Design development is a gradual process, translating your research visuals into silhouette, proportion, line, and detail. It is a state of mind where ideas are in flux and nothing is final. Be open to looking at your concept from different perspectives, recognizing false starts and possible changes in plan. Your concept should have room enough for you to move around in, selecting different aspects or themes for development, until you have found the one that offers you the greatest scope of design possibilities.

Think of your collection in groupings, or chapters of your theme, each one advancing a slightly different interpretation of your design story. Shorter attention spans and shifting fashion calendars call for directing your collection design into smaller, cohesive groups of five to seven looks built around a shared motif. Each can work as a mini-collection on its own while still evolving as part of one unified collection. Check your design plan to stay on track as you design.

Directional Adaptation

One way to begin evolving your conceptual ideas into a collection is by adapting your initial directional sketches. They hold your design vision, reflect your customer, and will jump-start your experimentation. Spin out variations through a run of silhouettes. Then start over, adapting another interpretation. It may take fifty or more trial sketches before your ideas begin to gel into a cohesive design message. However, if you are unable to move forward in developing the design ideas that first excited you, perhaps your theme should be set aside in favor of one that encompasses more opportunities for your design vision.

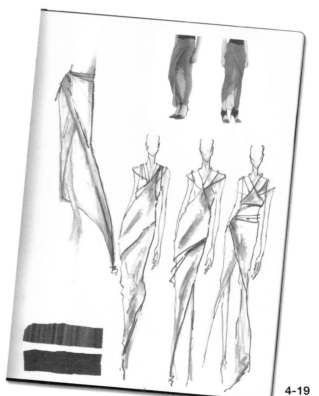

4-19 Luba Gnasevych spins out design variations from an initial directional image and sketch.

4-19

Silhouette

Silhouette and volume set the predominant character of a collection. By finding the influence for silhouette in your concept or theme visuals, you identify another effective starting point for design. Silhouette establishes a coherent working space that can hold your design message in context while you improvise proportion and line. For example, Naama Doktofsky adopts the triangle shape as a coherent framework for design development. She says, "This kept it simple and gave me a starting point for each piece."

Scale Variation

Use a focal element to unify collection designs by selecting a motif from your theme, such as a distinctive shape, print, detail, or embellishment. Play around with repeat variations of scale, repurposing your cohesive element throughout the range of pieces you are designing. Create balance and movement throughout your pieces by varying it in intensity and placement. Kate Lee originates a cohesive flow by interpreting her primary design motif, deep-sea cephalopod vents, in scale variations of fanned seaming, dimensional details, and pleats.

Designing Out of Abstraction

If you are translating an abstract idea or emotion into design, as Julie Rose Romano did a few pages back, you may want to explore different ways of finding potential shape and style lines in your visuals. Try drawing or tracing over the elements in an image and reconfigure them as silhouette and detail, layer them to discover variations, or combine shapes from several images as Xiao Lin does in evolving her quickly sketched designs. Your theme images should be rich in elements that can be adapted to style and seam lines, echoed in pattern and print, and rescaled into embroidery or embellishment design.

4-20

4-20 Wei Lin starts by creating linear abstractions as silhouettes, then explores proportion and construction on sketched trial overlays.

What Not to Do

- Overthink—focus on the details without seeing them as part of the whole design
- Overdesign—excessive use of any element; balance design intensity with simplicity
- Get too literal—avoid designs that imitate research too closely, are too derivative of trend or historical costume
- Lack coherence—incorporate design elements unrelated to your concept or theme
- Trying to analyze and create at the same time—interrupts the flow of inspiration; analyzing and creating are different mental processes

4-21

4-21 Naama Doktofsky.

4-22 Xiao Lin (right); Kate Lee (left).

4-22

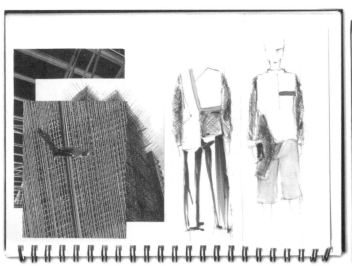

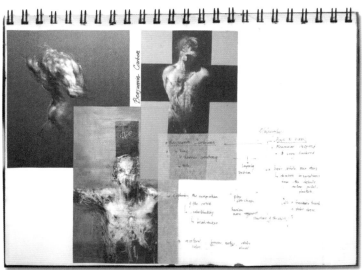

4-23 Matthew Harwoodstone's sketchbook development is based on big-city construction, inspiring, clean lines, and interesting shapes; his work is targeted upmarket but translatable for a mid-level customer.

 The more sophisticated a garment is, the easier and more intuitive it should be to wear.
—*Daniel Roseberry*

4-24 Peter Do's sketchbook development is characterized by artistic expression but grounded in design logic and merchandised for a luxury sportswear customer.

4-24

Designing Up

Whether classic or avant-garde, fashion design by its nature incorporates new, aspirational design ideas into collection, with couture as well as innovative high-end designers inspiring style for all other market level brands. In recent years the roles have often reversed, and the highly charged energy of commercial street style has influenced the runways of the haut monde. So regardless of your market or project criteria, you will be expected to bring a fresh point of view. For example, mainstream design teams will be looking for you to inject a higher aesthetic into their mass-market design strategies.

Market Guidelines for Design Development

Luxury market consensus

- Conceptually inspired development and personal artistic expression
- Directional looks evolving into a wearable lifestyle collection
- Full range of styles in varying degrees of design intensity, day to evening
- Free development improvised directly on the page in spontaneous, hand-drawn sketches, callouts, and luxurious quality fabrics
- Illustrative, proportional flats of select statement looks; schematics

Contemporary market consensus

- Aspirational interpretation of current runway ideas within brand aesthetic and budgetary constraints
- Seasonal deliveries organized by theme; sometimes designed seasonally, delivered monthly, each requiring themes and color stories
- Coordinated range of wearable pieces, career to casual to formal, with customer and sales guiding trend choice and design
- Hand-drawn sketch development, callouts, trending fabric and color
- Proportional flats with detail specifics and merchandising; schematics

4-25 "Dan" Yongeun Lee's sketchbook development brings a fresh point of view for his fall/winter portfolio collection.

4-25

4-26 Lauren Sehner translated her concept into runway reality through a combination of process draping and sketching.

4-27 Talisa Almonte used photos of her draped shapes for CSM (Central Saint Martins) White Project, drawing over, cutting up, and collaging to create new garment ideas.

4-26

 Keep it simple. Eliminate everything that interferes with the line. "

—*Cristobal Balenciaga*

Design Development Techniques

Designers think in shape, line, drape, and form and explore them using one or a combination of techniques:

- Process draping—direct dimensional trials in cloth on form
- Deconstruction/repurposing/collage—alternative techniques
- Process sketching—drawing design ideas directly on paper

4-27

4-28 Eugenia Sivilotti explores pattern and form, developing sketched ideas further through process draping trials. **4-28**

Process Draping

Process draping allows you to explore conceptual ideas dimensionally before translating them into sketch development or to prove your design ideas. Observing the potential shape, volume, and movement of fabric on the dress form can suggest variations and make it easier to build on your ideas. If you are working from design sketches, dimensional trials offer a way of testing the viability of your construction inventions. It is important to keep a photographic record of your draping trials for process analysis and to note variations in seaming or cut as suggestions for your next direction.

Deconstruction/Repurposing/Collage

Photo repurposing of a key research silhouette is another way to explore design variations. Working either directly on the image with pen line, as Talisa Almonte has done, or on trace overlays, draw new seam lines to make changes in silhouette, volume, or detailing. Deconstructing a photo of a garment silhouette by cutting and remixing the parts can provide fresh design innovations as well. The directional ideas you generate can then be spun off into related looks through sketching.

4-29 Peter Do explores design variations on the dress form, sketching and refining.

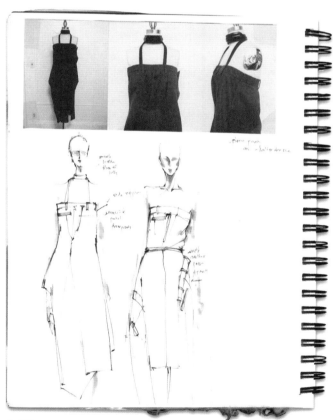

4-29

It's funny how a subtle shift in proportion can change something from classic to modern.

—*Karin Gustafsson, head designer, COS (Collection of Style)*

Process Sketching/Thumbnail Figures

Sketching makes sharing your design ideas possible. Your drawing technique, figure pose, and attitude all contribute to aesthetic and taste level. But the main focus of the process sketch is on the design, not the figure. The poses that serve your design message best are straightforward, connected to concept and sketched in consistent size and proportion. Figure expressiveness and mood can be conveyed simply through your ability to translate the look of your muse in a few quick strokes. If you are aiming for a sophisticated, upscale clientele but sketching your design ideas on quirky young figures, you are confusing your design message. As your concept and theme change with each seasonal collection, so the look of your muse should reflect the shift in mood and attitude.

4-30 Andreina Jiminez extracts shape and seaming from architecture plans. By manipulating web archive images in editing software, she creates new images, inspiring further designs.

4-30

4-31 Clockwise from top left: Jose Camacho (black color-pencil), Matthew Harwoodstone (black color-pencil), Sharon Rothman (90% gray color-pencil), Soo Bang (black color-pencil), and Peter Do (graphite pencil/ballpoint pen).

4-32 Clockwise from top left: Alexis Chung (eye shadow/black color-pencil), Luba Gnasevych (marker), Amanda Robertson (marker), and Alexis Chung (pencil/white paint).

Stylizing the Process Sketch

When sketching out your ideas, use a fresh, unforced line to stylize the total look. Draw the hand as a simple gesture and the face as an impression, not a depiction of features, with minimal mouth and hair. Stylize key accessories as suggestions for shape and relationship to figure. Your sketch style and technique should feel like an extension of yourself, in a medium or combination of media that feels the most natural to you: bold marker, fine-line marker, or a pencil line dark enough to hold its own on the page.

Each line style—crisp, sensitive, bold—tells the story of its designer and lends attitude to the sketch. Sure strokes indicate that you are practiced and confident in your process. A line that is searching or unsure may be whispery pale and difficult to see on the page. The use of tracing paper for pencil sketches invites smearing and faded lines and lowers the quality of your work. To make it easier to edit, keep your process sketch uncomplicated. It's not about how good you are at sketching, but how well you put your ideas across.

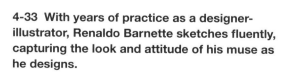

66 It's not about how good you are at sketching, but how well you put your ideas across. 99

4-33 With years of practice as a designer-illustrator, Renaldo Barnette sketches fluently, capturing the look and attitude of his muse as he designs.

4-33

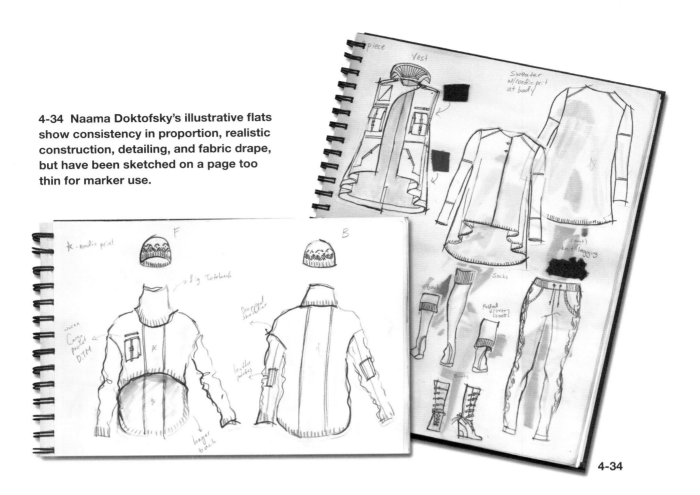

4-34 Naama Doktofsky's illustrative flats show consistency in proportion, realistic construction, detailing, and fabric drape, but have been sketched on a page too thin for marker use.

4-34

Process Sketching/Flats

Process flats and technical schematic sketches, such as pop-up diagrams, are another way of thinking through your design ideas and visualizing design specifics. They, too, should be quickly and cleanly sketched by hand, with correct detailing and a stylized attitude, in cylindrical perspective as if on an invisible dress form. Keep the line crisp, using minimal pale gray marker only when indicating a drop shadow, fabric drape, or garment interior. Process flats should demonstrate a proportion consistent with all the pieces in your groupings, as well as a correct understanding of garment construction.

Every design label has its own particular flats proportion for communicating garment specifications for production. By developing your own proportional templates, you make it easier to be consistent as you sketch your ideas and save time when you are immersed in designing. Many designers like working their flat designs over a full croquis figure template, drawn in correct flats proportion. Alternatively, flats templates can be created from flat croquis bodies, scanned and placed in vector applications on the computer. Used as under-drawings, templates ensure consistent garment silhouettes and are especially helpful when rescaling your rough designs from figure to flat format and vice versa. It is notoriously easy to lose the original silhouette and balance of detail in the transfer.

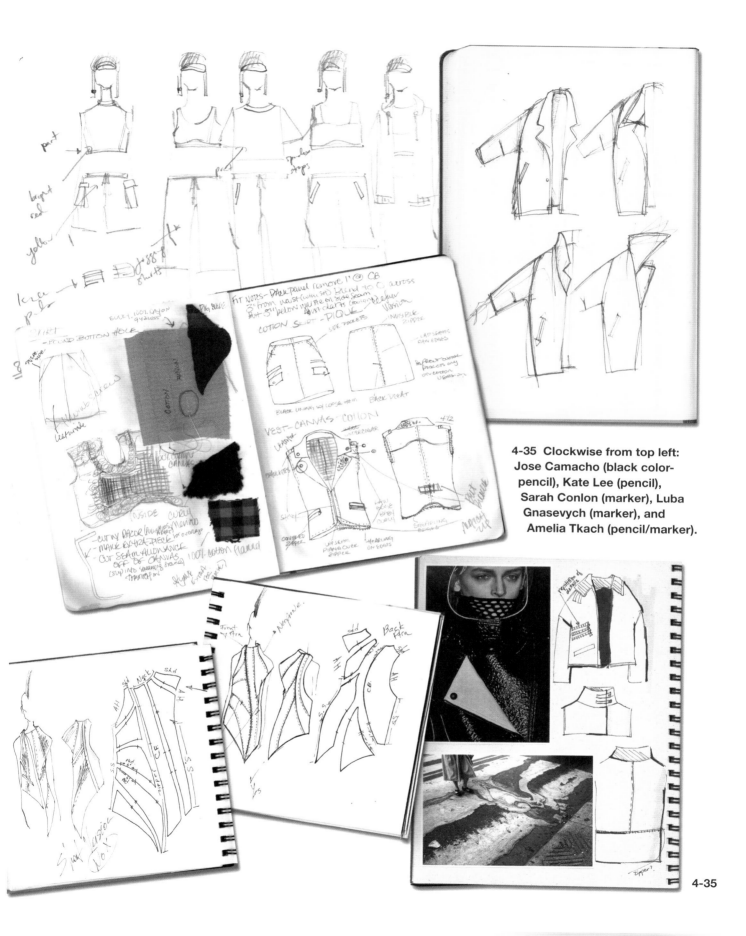

4-35 Clockwise from top left:
Jose Camacho (black color-
pencil), Kate Lee (pencil),
Sarah Conlon (marker), Luba
Gnasevych (marker), and
Amelia Tkach (pencil/marker).

4-35

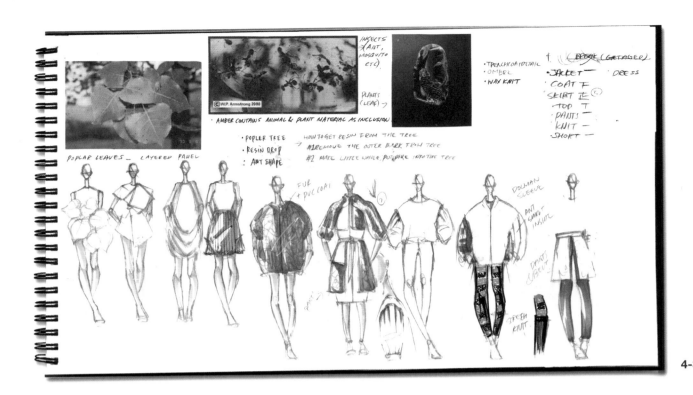

4-36

4-36 and 4-37 Jongah Lee's theme research provides several design paths to follow. She begins by envisioning a basic directional shape derived from each theme aspect. With design notes, images, and the merchandising list as guides, she sketches multiple design silhouettes and variations for her initial edit.

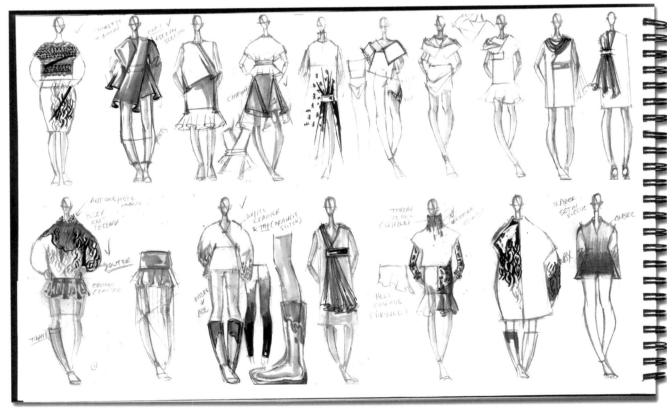

4-37

EXERCISE 11: Design Development

Part 1—Sketching Your Muse

Define one or two characteristics of your muse and explore stylizing her complete look as
you sketch.

- Pose a few simple figure variations in the attitude of your customer/muse.
  - One or two front views in variation (e.g., walking or legs together for pencil skirts; legs apart to show pant leg silhouette)
  - Back or side views to show relevant style lines/detail when needed
- Think runway—the straight-on walking pose, with models consistent in proportion and height.
- The arms and hands never cover important design details.
- Sketch directly on the page, or use templates beneath layout paper.

Part 2—Designing Variations on a Theme

- Design thirty or more looks that evolve your design direction through a single aspect of your theme.
- Vary scale and rhythm of silhouette and motif through your range of pieces.
- Develop the same number of looks through a second aspect of your theme, repeating similar variations using a different cohesive motif.
- Match selected images with each theme exploration, defining two groups.
- Note in callouts for each group the connections you are making between your silhouette/detailing ideas and your various thematic aspects.
- Compare the two groups objectively and find their common ground; can they be joined into one cohesive collection?

> **We become emotionally attached to what we do and it's hard to allow ourselves to let go of something. You have to sit back and look objectively at the whole collection piece by piece and ask some key questions.**
> —*Kieran Dallison*

The Edit: Shaping a Cohesive Collection

The essence of collection is editing—which of your looks to include, which to cut or refine, and how to integrate them into a unified whole. I have learned more about designing, and about myself, from the process of editing than any other aspect of design. Recognizing what doesn't work and why and realizing what changes need to be made require a shift in attitude, one that allows you to step back from your darlings, your individual designs, and see the collection they will become. Your combination of intuition, judgment, and objective analysis will shape your designs into a cohesive collection. This process comes together in a kind of alchemy, each decision changing the game and leading you to more design clarity. Your key questions: Do I need this piece to tell my design story? Does this piece fit in line? Does it have the same feeling? And perhaps the easiest to answer: Is the same woman wearing it?

As you begin, keep your design direction images in sight and your design plan or merchandising list at hand to guide your editing selections, as in Lynn Choi's sketchbook edit. Your next prerequisite is to put together a visual overview of your design sketches so that you can see all of them at one time in relation to each other, as Won Kim has done. Depending on how many sketches you have, you might want to work outside your sketchbook until you have edited them down to the semifinals.

4-38 Using simple shapes and complimentary colors, Won Kim plays with pattern placement as she edits with orange tape to mark her choices for her fall/winter collection.

4-38

Initial Edit

As a first step, select the looks you love and sort them visually into groups of companion designs—those that share design motif, silhouette, or style lines in repeat variation. You may want to copy your sketches and cut them out for greater flexibility in repositioning them. Once you see a viable group of designs coming together around a common conceptual focus, you will recognize if something is out of place or sending the wrong message. The clearer you are in your design direction and plan, the more uncomplicated it becomes—cut the looks that don't work, even if you love them. You can reinterpret them for another season.

4-39 Lynn Choi's evolution of shape is visually grouped for editing around common conceptual influences.

4-40 Jusil Carroll's inventive knitwear designs are grouped and swatched for editing.

4-39

4-40

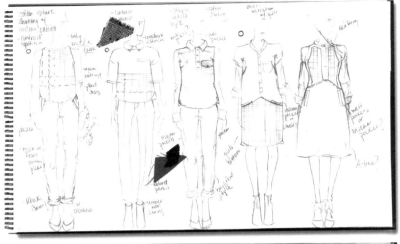

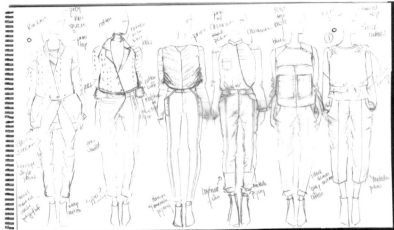

4-41 Rebecca Homen's traditional lineup of semifinalists are nearing final edit, with detailed callouts; color, fabric, and quilting flow is worked out carefully at this stage.

4-42 Sanly Yuen fills her pages with design ideas in quick, fluent sketches, marking the semifinalists in trial color.

4-41

4-42

The Semifinals

Your process sketchbook should contain a manageable number of development sketches, and your semifinal choices make the perfect sampling. To understand your own design thinking and clarify your selection process to others, it is crucial to see your full design progression, including:

- The looks you have earmarked for collection, clearly checked or identified
- The relevant designs you have rejected
- Notations of the changes you are planning for looks in flux

The sketches you include should be clear and fresh, whether you end up actually selecting all of them or not. Sanly Yuen's organic sketch development is one of many placement options you can experiment with as alternatives to a more traditional line-up, such as Rebecca Homen's heritage-inspired process style.

I have seen too many exciting sketchbooks fall flat in communicating the crucial process of editing. To focus your thinking, always include in your overview pages a few of the touchstone images that inspired your design ideas. When this visual link is missing, you are editing in a vacuum, and it will show in your choices. In an unfortunate demonstration of the axiom "What you see is what you get," the lack of workable editing materials in a sketchbook sends the message that no value has been placed on design experimentation or critical thinking. When sketches are faintly drawn in pencil on tracing paper, folded up and taped haphazardly into a sketchbook, there is no ardent involvement in the creative process.

4-43 Jordan Mayer's visual link to her colorful topographical inspiration, seen on page 7, comes across in a vivid flow of original prints in this semifinal edit for her Aerial portfolio collection.

4-43

> **Each group of distinctive design ideas relates to one another and depends on one another. And when you're telling a story on the runway, there has to be that kind of movement and flow.**
> —*Daniel Roseberry*

The Final Edit

Constructive critique calls for your focused attention on design concept as you refine your groupings into a balance of looks for a cohesive collection. Make sure that each grouping has a focal point and at least one statement look. If you can't decide, consult your "inner customer" and go by gut and intuition. Check your semifinalist choices objectively for adherence to theme and design plan. Compose a rhythmic flow of shape, silhouette, and style lines within your design criteria. Be prepared to weed out the looks that are redundant or not quite on message.

Calvin Klein was clear as crystal in his design aesthetic and vision. He simply eliminated everything that did not unmistakably express his design message, and whatever remained was right for collection. In evaluating your selections for final cut, expect to be recombining tops and bottoms; varying proportion of sleeve, skirt, or neckline; and adjusting concentration of detail. Solidify your collection by integrating your thumbnail groupings into one final cut, switching out a look when necessary or filling in with something new.

4-44 Daniel Silverstein edits for rhythm and balance of silhouette and detail for design continuity.

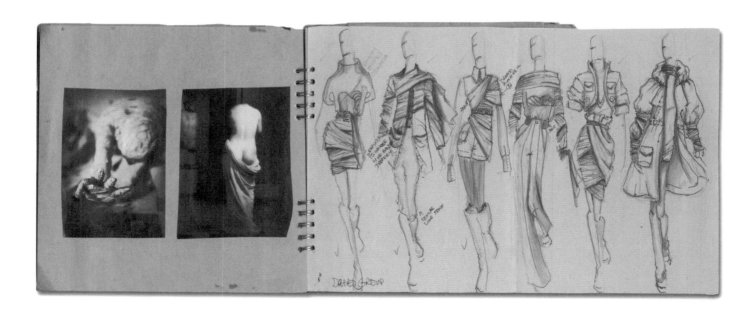

4-45 Ashley Gonzalez establishes a balanced flow of color, texture, and silhouette variation in this fall/winter grouping for her young contemporary customer.

Establishing Collection Flow

Your objective for final cut is to establish the flow of your collection—a natural progression of design continuity throughout the run of your designs. You will be synthesizing color and fabric with silhouette as major players in your design story. The way you arrange them, in waves of visual rhythm, affects the emotional response of your buyer and advances your design story to resolution. It gives your collection life and balance and creates flow. And, as in music or storytelling, a pause in the flow of a collection carries a lot of weight.

- Take it down—produce a visual pause using design simplicity or receding color/value.
- Ease it up—create drama using design intensity or contrast, bold embellishment, or color pops.

Look to the masters for examples—Valentino, Giorgio Armani—and experiment for yourself. Move through the composition of your collection, pausing where you want to adjust the tempo of your story, focusing attention on your innovative ideas, and emphasizing a standout design. The eye will follow the path you create.

> 66 The eye will follow the path you create. 99

Sketchbook Editing Techniques

Before making your final decisions on color and fabric placement, test variations in design sequence for your final collection by using your pre-cut thumbnail sketches, repositioning them until you are satisfied. You may want to lead off with your most directional or innovative design as a statement look to introduce the companion designs that follow and finish with a strong finale. Or adopt a lifestyle approach, with day/career looks in the lead, followed by a transition into evening wear.

Once you have decided your collection sequence, print out multiple copies of your finalized sequence in black and white line for use as blank templates for your color and fabric trials. Experiment and recolor until you get a few different colorways for each look or grouping. As you make your choices and work out your final color and fabric flow, make sure that your core colors and fabrics form a connecting thread. This stage is reality-check time, when last-minute changes are common and everything comes together, sometimes in surprising ways.

In your sketchbook, render the flow of color and detail quickly, with a light touch, to clearly define and preserve the creative freshness of the design process. Your final cut should always be characterized by the placement of fabric swatches for each look, a clear color story, and at least one visual touchstone tying it to theme. With all decisions made and design vision finalized into a collection, you have achieved your process sketchbook goal and are ready to begin translating the spontaneity of your creative process into presentation format.

4-46 and 4-47 Both Naama Doktofsky (opposite) and Lynn Choi (below) work smart, using b/w copies of their semifinal edits as templates for color trials. Note the balance of silhouette, proportion, and color in Naama's cohesive design variations. Fabric snips help Lynn establish a rhythmic flow of color and intensity in her design sequence.

4-47

4-48 Chance Thach mixes two thematic influences into one design concept for spring/summer final cut. He carries poppy red throughout in a balanced rhythm of prints and solids, linked by pinks and earthy plums. A fabric story with a more cohesive base would provide wearable and textural variety.

4

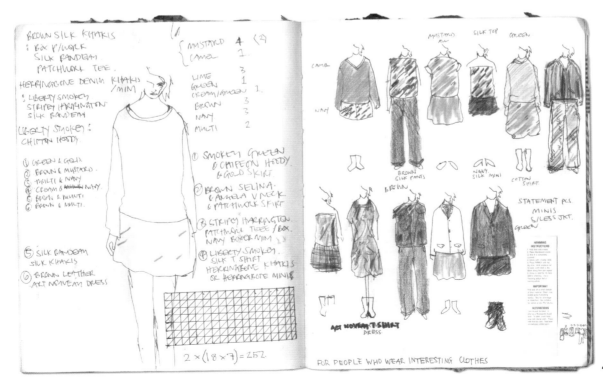

4-49

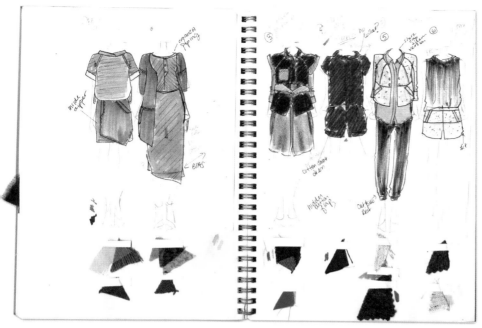

4-50 Rebecca Homen's smart editing strategy balances the flow of silhouette and coordinating pieces for her final cut, integrating two possible groupings or deliveries with a base of gray that allows for cross-pollination.

4-51 Xiao Lin's Art Specialization Critic's Award–winning project focuses on modern art in her final cut. After realizing her collection needed a wider range of functional pieces, she reedited to include more coordinates.

4-50

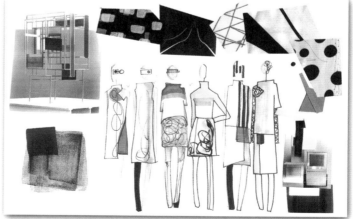

4-49 Luke Hall grounds his eclectic mix of "interesting clothes" with clear direction and specifics for producing his CSM thesis look book collection, well edited for balance and flow of color and pattern.

4-51

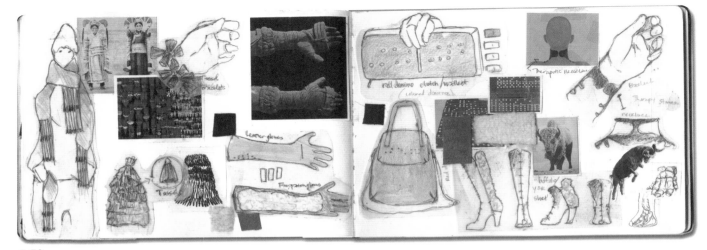

Creative Extras

Accessories are a natural extension of your design vision and expand job opportunities by showcasing another aspect of your design talent. Offering a great boot, must-have bag, statement print scarf, or hand-knit hat creates excitement in styling your looks. If you design accessories well and have something new to say, include them as companion pieces for your collection, tying them into your theme motif and color story. Your design ideas should be cleanly sketched with associated research visuals and fabric, showing an understanding of proportion, dimensional perspective, and basic construction.

If you are inspired to explore original print design, gather your inspirational images and ideas and create variations of prints that coordinate with your collection and unify your color story. Experiment in any medium from watercolor to computer software, or combine them. Print your designs on fabric for collection swatches or yardage for scarves and wraps.

4-53 Kieran Dallison.

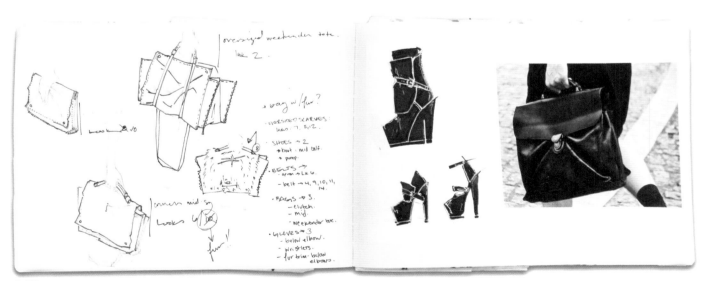

EXERCISE 12: Collection Edit

Part 1—Initial design selection for your semifinal edit

- Gather key research elements, color, fabric story, design plan materials, and fifty to eighty design sketches (figures or flats).
- Copy your sketches and cut them out so you can move them around in trial placements for more visual flexibility.
- Begin by selecting the designs you love—but be willing to cut or make changes for the good of the collection.
- Judge the ability of your designs to convey concept and theme.
- Make selections based on customer expectations and lifestyle necessities, market guidelines, and merchandising plan goals.

Part 2—Semifinal critique

- Observe how your semifinalists sort themselves into clusters of related elements (the beginnings of collection and delivery).
- Getting to the final cut requires varying the rhythm and intensity of a cohesive design motif within the group relationship.
- Expand or cut designs to meet your intended design plan.
- Make sure your range of pieces meets your merchandising criteria.

Part 3—The final cut

- Complete an overview or line-up of your final cut, establishing the flow of your design story and finalizing the placement and sequence of looks in your comprehensive collection.
- Print out multiple copies of your final black and white line-up; use this for color/fabric trials.
- Finalize the flow of color, texture, and pattern through your integrated groupings.
- In your sketchbook, adjust the pace and flow of your design story in the line-up, lightly indicating color, fabric texture, and pattern.
- Attach actual fabric swatches for each look; combine theme visuals with sketched designs to define your vision.

Chicago native Lauren Sehner earned her BFA from FIT in 2012, winning the Mark Waldrop Critic's Award for Design Excellence in fall 2009 and the Geoffrey Beene/CFDA Scholar Award in spring 2011. She concurrently participated as a finalist for the CFDA Scholarship competition, Gilt Groupe/CFDA All-Star, and Elle Fashion Next Scholarship on the runway at Lincoln Center. Internships for Phillip Lim and Calvin Klein Collection and freelance design posts led to her present role as assistant designer for Adam Lippes.

4-54

LAUREN SEHNER

What guides your sketchbook decisions?

Sketchbooks are all about helping you understand what you're doing, keeping it clear for you. And then the presentation sketchbook makes it all readable. I start by thinking about my customer—women who inspire me, women I hope will wear my clothes. I think I speak a lot more strongly visually than I do verbally and the images are all carefully chosen to convey associations. I always keep a color page together with fabrics for a direct correlation. My thesis sketchbook was a good tool for me and I used it to play with layout and plan out how I would treat my actual portfolio.

What do you consider when editing a collection?

I think editing is always a tough process, because when you design you like everything. They're your babies, so you find importance in all of them. But I always ask someone whose opinion I respect, someone who understands my aesthetic and customer. You have to find looks that are key for you—the looks that helped tell your story. Which are the crucial pieces and which are supporting? Which looks help push your collection along? And then there are the pieces that help make the collection balanced . . . .

How do you decide on sequence as you finalize your color and fabric?

I like to keep the looks in groups. There are usually a few stories within the larger collection story. I look for similarities in design and silhouette. I want to keep similar fabrics together. What looks good together on a page matters—balancing color and linear details and embellishments.

See Lauren Sehner's video interview and sketchbook tour online at www.bloomsbury.com/rothman-fashion-sketchbook

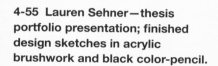

❝ I think editing is always a tough process, because when you design you like everything. ❞

4-55 Lauren Sehner—thesis portfolio presentation; finished design sketches in acrylic brushwork and black color-pencil.

STUDY

25

LAUREN SEHNER

30

4-55

Originally from Massachusetts, Matthew Harwoodstone majored in fashion design at FIT and in 2013 was selected for Art Specialization and represented FIT for Fusion, a runway competition between FIT and Parsons students. He was a finalist for the Geoffrey Beene/CFDA Scholarship competition and the Tory Burch Mentorship Program in 2014. His internship experience was with Jen Kao and Jonathan Simkhai before graduating with a BFA in spring 2015.

4-56

MATTHEW HARWOODSTONE

Where do you find your inspiration?

I've always loved architecture, so a lot of the time I look at the spaces I'm in, whether it's a great building in New York or the Arizona desert, which is a new inspiration for my next collection. It's whatever I'm feeling about them. But I'm careful to choose something that isn't too specific or restricting for me as I design, something with enough inspiring elements to actually work from and create a vibe. I take my own photos and get conceptual connections between shape and form and the more abstract ideas I get from them. I also look at the major modeling agencies to see their new faces, so I'm creating a look that is new and different.

How do you begin your design process?

As I begin a collection, I have benchmarks in mind to keep me on track and the collection in balance. Before I start developing my designs, I like to sketch a few ideas and associate them with images. I think how I might pull design from them and play with the lines to create my design direction. I choose colors and add fabrics at this stage. Feeling the fabric helps me think about how I'll be using it and if I'll be able to construct and produce the garment.

> " For me, the sketchbook is as important as the final project. It helps initiate all my ideas. "

Do you think about putting your sketchbook together as you design?

For me, the sketchbook is as important as the final project. It helps initiate all my ideas. So sometimes when I'm laying out the images, I spend the time to experiment with positioning, because I know it will help me in designing the clothes. Some of my design lines actually come from the shapes I've created in my page layouts. So, I really think of it as a full-page effect.

See Matthew Harwoodstone's video interview and sketchbook tour online at www.bloomsbury.com/rothman-fashion-sketchbook

4-57 For his senior thesis collection, Matthew Harwoodstone blends his sensitive design sketches with digital techniques, preserving and intensifying the feeling in his originals.

4-57

The sketchbook is one of the most important ways for the industry to see how the designer interprets inspiration through conceptual thinking, design inventions and rough development, fabrication and construction.

—*Christopher Uvenio,* Vogue Italia *designer, teacher*

CHAPTER 5
PRESENTATION SKETCHBOOK

Your presentation sketchbook is the fearlessly informal companion to your polished collection portfolio. Together they represent your point of entry to your future career and should showcase your very best design talents, each in its own way. Although it is a presentation version of your process sketchbook, it should share the same creative breath as the original and most of the same content—a cleaner, more organized version of your personal design style. With consistent sequence and a few smart presentation strategies, even mediocre designs can make an impression.

Once you have your collection in the final cut stage, you are ready to concentrate on editing and branding your content. Most likely you are clearer about your aesthetic and design vision, because they have evolved through your creative experience. Looking back, you might welcome the chance to adjust your images and sketches to show creative growth and highlight how you arrived at your collection. Your presentation sketchbook offers the opportunity to rethink the way you communicate your design ideas. It can be used to refine brand aesthetic and experiment with trial compositions and sequencing for your portfolio.

5-1 Amelia Tkach designs with a standout sense of color and fabric for the "contemporary, eco-conscious customer." In her job search sketchbook, she demonstrates strong merchandising skills, placing flats and fabric in context with her working sketches, and adds diagrams and callouts for clear communication.

5-1

Presentation Sketchbook Considerations

Your sketchbook for presentation will accompany your portfolio on professional interviews or be submitted for project or juried competition. It will be handled by many people over time and possibly continue to function as your sketchbook in ongoing design development. Look for a standard sewn binding or spiral-bound book with hard covers and sturdy pages. Check the basic sketchbook options and criteria, outlined in *Chapter 4*, and consider the possibility of extending your collection aesthetic to your choice of book for a standout presentation.

 It is your thoughts, your strengths and your own perspective, as showcased in your sketchbook, that will make you unique and a standout among the crowd.
—*Sonja Nesse*

5-2 **Luke Hall's sketchbook attracts with its unusual color and enticing bulk, bursting with design ideas. He chose a standard book, sturdily bound and covered to withstand lots of use.**

5-2

Presentation Sketchbook Format Options

Portfolio companion

- Ideally, this sketchbook should match your portfolio in format and aesthetic. Functionally, it should be the same size or slightly smaller. Its covers can be skillfully altered to harmonize with your individual aesthetic and meet the standard for professional skill and ease of handling.

Competition or small project

- Most project sketchbooks will be one-collection versions of the full portfolio companion book.

Handcrafted sketchbook

- Great care must be taken in executing this type of sketchbook, as there is a fine line between handcrafted and "crafty." Its pages must turn easily and lay flat when opened, as a fully functional sketchbook would, and it should not need its own protective case. However, you can create a case or folio to accommodate both portfolio and sketchbook as one presentation.

Formal booklet

- If your brief requires you to present a formal version of your process, your sketchbook pages can be software composed, printed, and professionally bound with soft covers to create a clean, flat presentation, easily contained in a project box or folio. The booklet is a virtual version of the sketchbook without the authenticity of the original.

5-3

5-3 Peter Do (top pages) covered his competition sketchbook with paint-spattered leather to match his collection theme and design aesthetic and won the CFDA Scholarship; Jusil Carroll (center left), Daniel Silverstein (center right), and Anya Zelinska (below) branded their sketchbook covers to reflect their portfolio collection aesthetic—perforated leather, fossilized fish, and signature blue rose, respectively.

5-4 Kate Lee's sleekly bound covers (right) hold composite layouts of her spontaneous sketchbook process for competition; Anthony Argentina (below) created a memorable hand-painted folio for his competition sketchbook and presentation.

5-4

Content Edit for Presentation Sketchbook

A polished presentation is contradictory to the nature and purpose of a sketchbook. Smoothing over your unique rough edges, where the gold shines through, runs counterintuitive to the creative process. But if *all* your edges are rough, it can be difficult to see the real glimmers. This sketchbook is not about recreating your process as presentation but about cleaning up any messes, editing through excess content, adding notations, and identifying and preserving the flow of your design story to make it readable. It is a second chance to show your ability to organize and edit your own process—how you gather your glimmers to create the gold of a cohesive collection.

Designers want to be inspired, love ideas, and look to you to show them new ways of seeing the ordinary and creative ways of interpreting research. They are drawn to a sketchbook full of evocative images, rich colors, and textural fabrics, elements that extend your creativity into the world beyond your book. But what if your process sketchbook is so full of ideas and inspiration that the thread of your design process gets lost in pages and pages of ideas? Even the most dedicated sketchbook viewers need a bit of path-clearing to help them through it.

You can control what you reveal by editing and remixing the flow of your process to emphasize your best ideas and strongest looks while easing back on the rest. Since each of us has a completely individual combination of strengths and limitations, it will be up to you to identify objectively what you need. If you include too much that is visually off-concept or irrelevant, you are sending the same visual message about your design focus. If you include compelling conceptual images but show few development sketches, you may be perceived as strong in concept but weaker in design.

5-6

5-5 **In these portfolio companion sketchbook pages, Koon Lim takes us from original inspiration through richly fabricated working sketches and notes to finished art, and his Critic Award–winning graduate runway show look.**

5-6 **Chanan Reifen's thesis sketchbook, filled with design and knit-down inventions, contains the edited process for his Critic Award–winning knitwear in FIT's Future of Fashion 2015 graduate runway show.**

> **I am a maker, not an illustrator. I design not only to put ideas forward, but to make them a reality.**
>
> —*Luke Hall, design director, Ann Taylor/LOFT*

What to Leave In and What to Take Out

Your mobile design studio remains the place for your personal process, the home of your late-night trials that went nowhere, the pages of dye formulas and moments of frustration, expletives on pages and sketches scribbled out. These are all vital parts of your personal process, but not all are necessary to your professional viewers, who are searching for the gold.

As you revisit the pages of your process sketchbook, choose the best of your design story as you edit—the pages that show your design plan as it evolved, the creative moments that clicked and were developed into your collection—but don't cut too deeply and leave out the ideas and experiments you love that didn't make it to final cut. Keep your imperfect little sketch on a napkin and the weird

idea you had for a neck brace; they may be exactly what will show something new and fresh. Keep the best of your design plans and merchandising notes, but if you have six pages of butterfly research, think about editing it.

Reviewing the Process Sketchbook Content List (*Chapter 4*):
- What is missing in your content as you go into presentation?
- What adjustments in the visual flow will tell your story better?

The graphic strategies and spatial dynamics suggested on the following pages will help you represent your creative process in a presentation-worthy sketchbook that retains all the spontaneity of the original and feels as lovingly worked on.

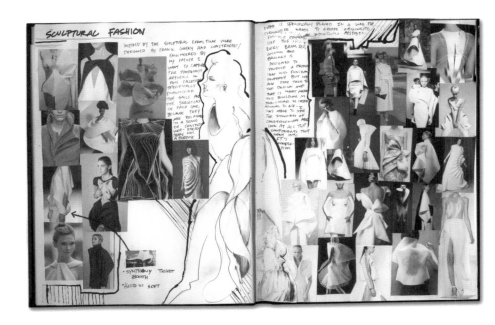

5-7 Jordan Mayer designs a striking double-spread layout connecting her most inspiring research into concept, united by a central sketch and notations.

5-8 Luke Hall's sketchbook is an eclectic mix of influences: grunge, middle-class crafty, and early twentieth-century artistry. Pages of ideas and design plans guide his process of development, and line-up variations evolve into a thoughtfully edited collection.

> **You want to get a real job in a real marketplace that makes real clothes, so your design direction and callouts are a good indication that you are actually thinking design.**
> —*Naama Doktofvsky, designer, Shoshanna*

Content Presentation

Your purpose for using the presentation sketchbook is a deciding factor in how you present it. Whether for portfolio, project, or competition, your design thinking and individual point of view need to come across clearly and strongly.

The Portfolio Companion Sketchbook shows the guts of your creative process. It should be lightly edited to preserve as much relevant process as possible, showcasing your creativity in action and your ability to cleanly organize your ideas into collection. Titles should show your viewer the way in and through your process and define your creative thinking; callouts should be clearly readable.

5-9 Luba Gnasevych's design studio sketchbook preserves the guts of her design process, with strong visual metaphors, working sketches, fabrication, and technical diagramming.

5-9

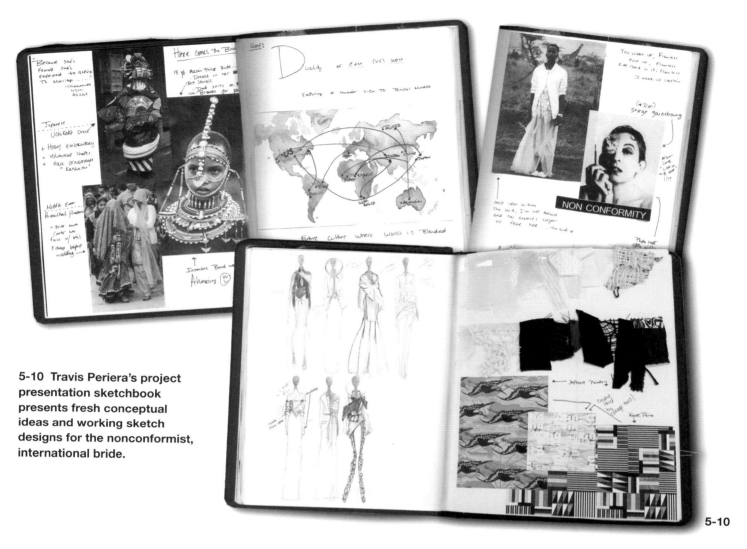

5-10 Travis Periera's project presentation sketchbook presents fresh conceptual ideas and working sketch designs for the nonconformist, international bride.

5-10

The Project Presentation Sketchbook criteria are the same as for *The Portfolio Companion Sketchbook*, but dedicated only to one specific project and its requirements. No additional material gathered or sketched for other projects should be included. It is a slightly more edited version of your original, hands-on process—neat and clean, but still informal and as close to being authentic as possible.

The Competition Presentation Sketchbook is usually a more formally designed version of your process sketchbook content and often contains software-composed page layouts and mood/concept pages. It is not polished; however, attention is paid to organization and logical sequence, clean fabrication, titles in print, and a concisely worded vision statement, all according to specific submission guidelines. It is your authentic process, once removed.

5-11

5-11 For her portfolio companion sketchbook, Naama Doktofsky compiles her final color edit trials, showing her upmarket lifestyle aesthetic as "effortless luxury, combining the raw and natural with the glamorous and refined."

Matching Job Market with Presentation Style

One of the marks of a professional designer is to know your own aesthetic and clearly embody it in everything you do. Your brand aesthetic is a natural extension of your design philosophy and the key to creating instant recognition for yourself as a designer. It should be evident in the visual direction and style of your presentation sketchbook, the same personal style that sets your designs apart. If you are on target, the professional critic or talent director viewing your sketchbook will know at a glance if you understand their aesthetic and customer. They will see if you have fresh design ideas that will strengthen their brand and if your design choices reflect relevant market considerations.

The awful truth is that no matter how innovative and spot on your design ideas are, the way you place them on the page becomes the aesthetic message you send. It projects your design persona and can make all the difference in how your work is received and understood. Even if your design aesthetic matches your page placement, the folks at Jil Sander will not respond as well to a quirky, collaged sketchbook style as they will to a clean, well defined, minimalist way of working. However, the same approach with a different aesthetic might get a second look at Marni.

5-12 and 5-13 Kieran Dallison's job search sketchbook reflects his vision, "a global-minded mix of local traditions filtered through a distinctly American sensibility," in a content flow that includes inspiration, conceptual thinking, and working sketches.

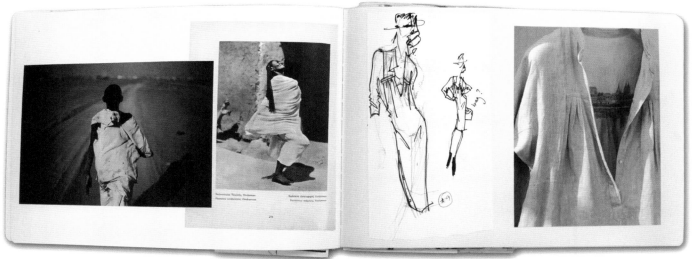

5-13

Less is more . . . let the texture and visual content speak for themselves. I find that creative people have an innate aesthetic sense or eye for what fits and what doesn't. Listen to your inner eye.

—Claudine Calabrese, Claudine Calabrese Design

Graphic Strategies for Presentation

Your goal for your creative work is to be taken seriously and considered on a professional level, or as close to it as possible. You always want to make it easy for the design professionals who view your sketchbook to stay focused on your talent without being distracted by the mechanics of a fold or annoyed by having to rotate your book in order to see your designs. Graphic design strategies offer ways to raise the quality of your design process above the realm of the school project and give you an easy advantage. They can seem simple and obvious once you begin to utilize them, but they should not be overlooked.

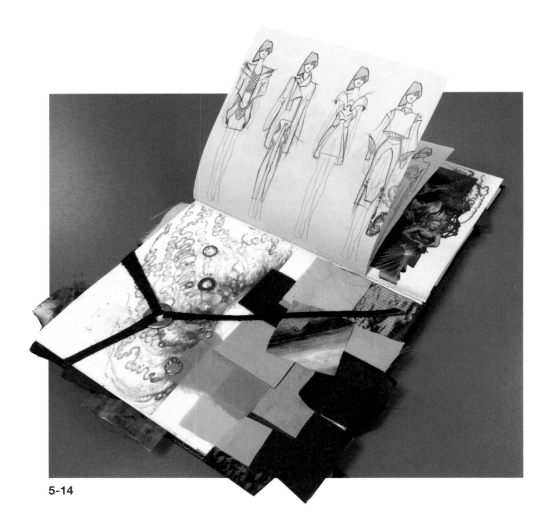

5-14

5-14 Neda Sharafi creates a standout competition sketchbook by cleverly juxtaposing theme imagery, working sketches, fabric, and color palette in one glance.

Synchronizing Your Aesthetic Message

By using your innate aesthetic sense even in your most spontaneous moments of inspiration, experimentation, and development, you show authenticity. By synchronizing your aesthetic message with your target market on the title page of your presentation sketchbook, you show that you understand the importance of first impressions in framing your essential style. It is your viewer's first contact and marks the entry to your design world. Begin the visual sequencing of your design story by putting your aesthetic forward strongly on your very first page.

5-15 Four strong title pages express designer aesthetic and introduce a collection: Sanly Yuen (top), Sharon Rothman (center), Eugenia Sivilotti (below left), and Naama Doktofsky (below right).

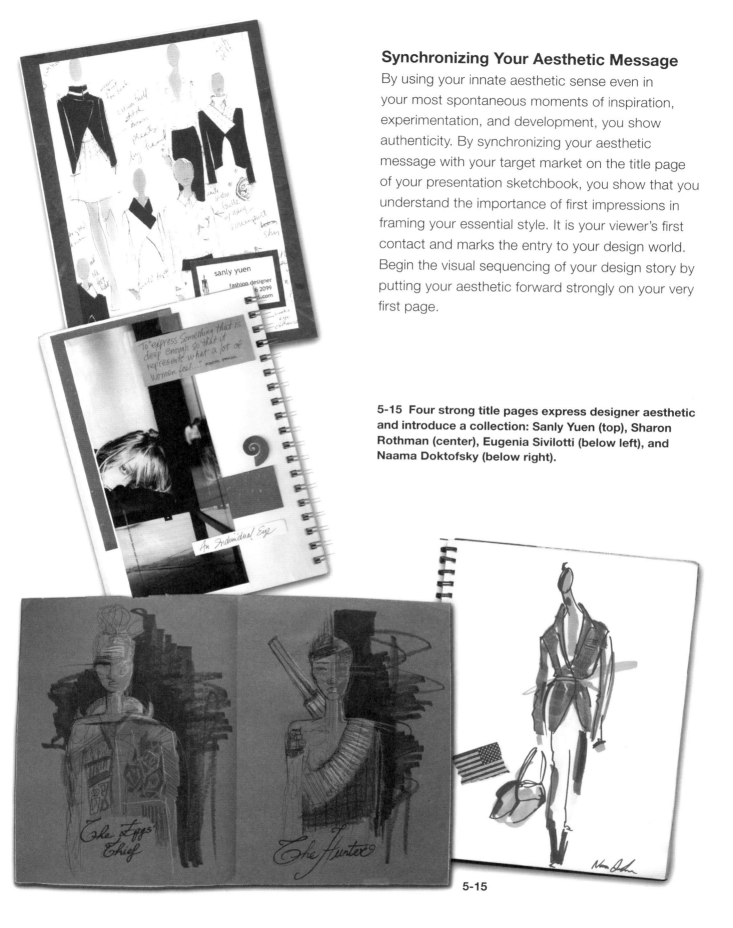

5-15

Content Flow

You can plan the visual flow of your presentation sketchbook in the same way you established the rhythm and sequence of your collection. As you edit through your pages, adjust the tempo and continuity of your process to highlight your natural strengths. Your fabrics can be given their own dedicated spread along with images that tell your directional color story. But to add richness and textural excitement to your process and to focus on your design thinking, consider integrating key swatches and fabric manipulations, concept images, and readable callouts with your sketches as you develop your designs. Flats and construction schematics can accompany your sketches whenever you want to show your inventiveness with a different way of cutting or creating shape.

By putting your pages together in your own unique way with consistent concept, color, and mood, as Lisa Almonte has achieved in her CFDA Scholarship Competition sketchbook, you will show that you can maintain your design focus through all stages of the process. Consult your design plan and market guidelines in deciding how to compose and remix your elements for your best presentation—where to place your flats, where and how to include fabric compositions, when to focus on merchandising.

5-16

5-16 Lisaneyla Almonte's exquisite mix of working sketch, theme imagery, and luxury fabrication creates a flow of content that matches her design aesthetic and art skills.

Extending the Page

It is essential to see the full run of your design development ideas together on your sketchbook pages to visually judge design flow and collection cohesion during editing and at the final cut stage. Attaching a foldout to your page is one way to effectively extend your horizontal space and must be carefully planned. But don't assume that your viewer will know to open it. I have missed seeing pivotal collection sketches many times, because there was no indication on the sketchbook page that a foldout was there to open. Consider as well that refolding an accordion fold can be tricky while trying to stay focused on a candidate's design process.

If you decide to add a foldout, keep it simple, short, and practical:

- Limit your extension to one page (extends a double spread into three pages).
- Unfold to the right, as the pages turn in format.
- Use the same paper weight as your book page, never flimsy or sheer.
- Attach with clear tape strongly and cleanly for a flat fold.
- Don't leave a foldout "cover" blank: place an image or label and indicate the opening edge.

5-17 Lynn Choi's well-designed foldout is constructed with quality paper, reflecting her high design aesthetic. But because her full line-up unfolds beyond what you see here, it has proven unwieldy at job interviews.

5-17

Spatial Dynamics

The principles and elements of design are, in reality, how we navigate visually through any space or format. They are fundamental to creating anything, and therefore apply to all aspects of design, for example, architectural, industrial, fashion, and graphics. Even in your most spontaneous sketchbook pages, your design ideas should always be the main focus within your composition. Mood and inspiring images play supporting roles and give your designs conceptual context. By understanding the dynamics of spatial relationship, you can focus attention on your designs simply by adjusting your elements on the page.

❝ Your design ideas should always be the main focus within your composition. ❞

5-18 Paola Bueso-Vadell's free-form, swirling pen lines connect her double spread pages into one continuous flow of color, pattern, and linear fancy.

5-19 Sharon Rothman sketches layouts for double spread continuity, trying out different ways to show feeling and aesthetic. Luxurious lace (above) prompts dreamlike flights of fancy, while with a cleaner aesthetic (below) an imagined breeze creates movement that unites the pages into one composition.

5-19

Double Spread/Single Composition

Your sketchbook is a progression of double spreads, or pairs of facing pages, each pair seen as one working space. From a lifetime of reading books and magazines, we are conditioned to ignore the gutter, or binding, between them. We visually connect the content on both sides. So whatever elements you place on one page can relate to the other as one composition by connecting them in movement, color, or balance of space. Sketching different layout ideas for double spread continuity is the designer's way of working out visual expressions of theme and aesthetic, triggering creative solutions.

Page Layout

An awareness of spatial relationships helps you see your own work more objectively. As you experiment with trial placements of designs and images, fabric, and notations in your double spread, sense that some appear more solid in volume and density, while others have a lighter, softer feeling. For example, positioning large fabric swatches above the heads of fine-line design sketches can visually overwhelm them. Heavier elements create visual stability and are best placed lower on your pages, grounding the lighter elements, which feel instinctively in balance when placed higher on the page.

Each design concept has its own personality. To find the layout best suited to yours, first place your elements by eye and by intuition. Then begin to think design. Try balancing elements of varying weights and volumes, and play around with repeats of figures or geometric shapes in smaller and larger scales. Judge your own best aesthetic proportion using page layout, just as you would when designing the elements of a garment.

5-20 Klara Olsson skillfully balances vibrant color with dynamic theme images, using negative space and visual direction to unite her double spread composition. Note how the upward dynamic of the bird helps lift the weight of fabric above.

5-20

5-21 Matthew Harwoodstone (top) develops the look of his androgynous muse, consciously balancing the page with his sketches, and carrying the eye from research to sketch to the callouts that inform the negative space. Sarah Conlon (below) uses negative space and the repetition of shape and imagery to convey her message through page layout, connecting fabric and muse with mood and concept.

5-21

Negative Space

Rules of composition don't always apply across the board when you are working spontaneously in your sketchbook. Respecting the space on a page helps make good layouts intuitive. Our innate ability to see the shape of the space between objects, or negative space, is how we judge proportion and balance. Translate this to your sketchbook by training your eye to see the space surrounding your elements as a shape itself. By varying this negative space in size and shape, you can balance the spatial proportion in your double spread layout and the visual progression of your sketchbook contents.

Look at art or coffee table books for layout ideas that resonate with your aesthetic and design story; search out blogs for interesting graphic critiques to spark ideas.

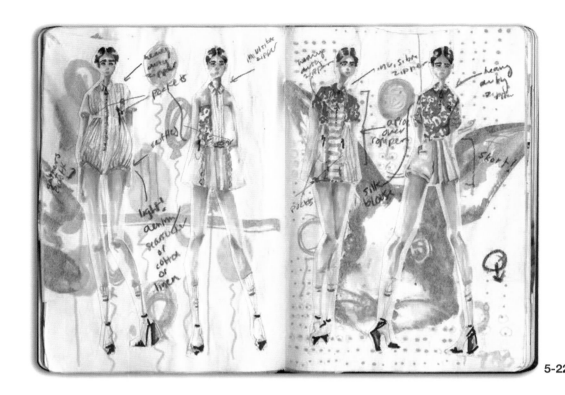

5-22

5-22 The bold size and color of Taylor Ormond's hand-painted backgrounds overwhelm her charming designs, even through the translucent layer.

5-23 Taylor's second project uses one manipulated theme image to support her designs; by placing it lower than her design details, she allows negative space to frame her creativity.

5-23

Backgrounds and Graphics

The simplicity of negative space is the showcase of choice for creative design. A frame of clear space removes all distractions and allows silhouette to stand out and originality to shine. Decorative elements, backgrounds, and diverse graphics can have the opposite effect unless used with a light touch and practiced eye. In a field of competing visual messages, your all-important sketch details are easily lost. The activity, intensity, and placement of distracting elements can overwhelm them, confuse silhouette, camouflage fabric swatches, and change the impact of color. On the other hand, simple, relevant graphics can unify your design process and support your creative vision. By keeping background drama minimal, you free up negative space on the page. Even excellent designs will take on the taste level and aesthetic of their presentation.

5-24 Kate Lee (top right) uses graphic elements with a light touch to suggest and echo her repeating curved-vent motif. In three carefully positioned images, Lauren Sehner (below) explains her concept from abstract idea to design, framing her key directional sketch.

TORQUE

24

SPINNING **CLASSICISM** WITH CLASSIC DESIGN

TO CREATE SOMETHING COMPLETELY **MODERN**

STUDY

LAUREN SEHNER

5-24

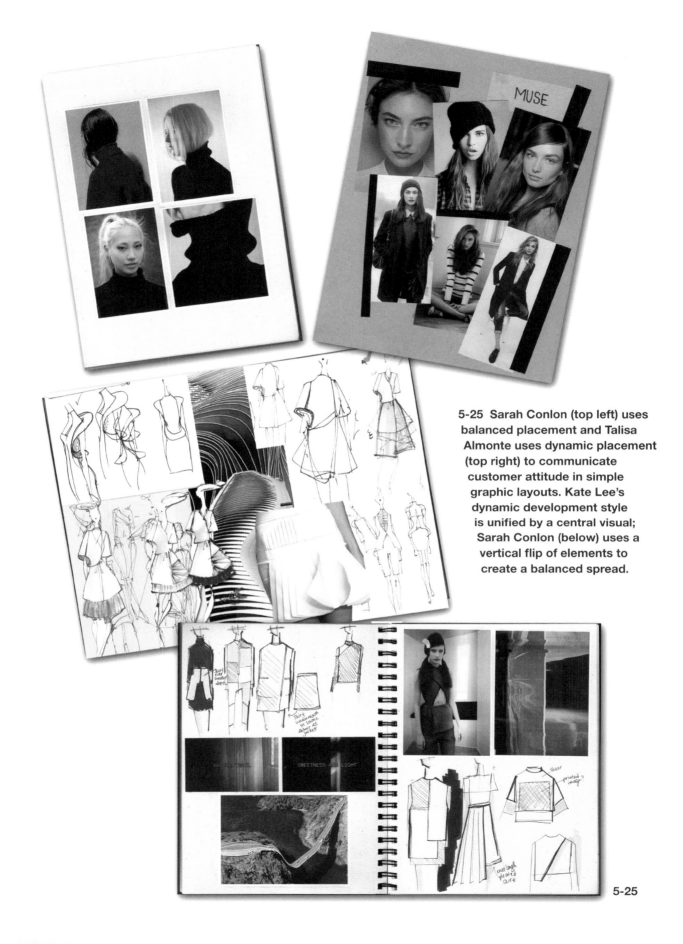

5-25 Sarah Conlon (top left) uses balanced placement and Talisa Almonte uses dynamic placement (top right) to communicate customer attitude in simple graphic layouts. Kate Lee's dynamic development style is unified by a central visual; Sarah Conlon (below) uses a vertical flip of elements to create a balanced spread.

5-25

Visual Direction

Like direction for film, direction for any sequential presentation communicates mood and aesthetic and creates movement throughout your pages. For example, the visual metaphors you have used to link your concept images to the fabric or design ideas they inspired carry your design sketches forward as you develop the flow of your ideas. It is game changing when you realize that by shifting the position of a few elements on your pages, you can influence the way your work is perceived. You can bring a static page to life and save your ideas from being lost among competing elements.

Direct your own creative energy, and the eye of the viewer, by consciously arranging your elements in simple, visually directed layouts—a resonant image, vibrant color, touchable fabric, kinetic lines, or directed gesture. Experiment and compare your own versions of these three different basic layouts:

- Balanced placement creates unity and easy communication.
- Dynamic placement creates energy and movement using asymmetry and active lines.
- The center is where the eye looks first, the target placement for your key designs and ideas. Placing elements in corners will scatter attention away from center stage.

5-26 Neda Sharafi illustrates the visual power of center position, further targeting her designs within a circular graphic field.

5-26

The working sketch is all about the details, the specifics of design, fabrics, drape, top stitch . . . taking it from concept to production.

—*Renaldo Barnette, fashion designer, illustrator, teacher*

The Working Sketch

The working sketch represents a stage of design communication somewhere between the rough process sketch and a finished presentation sketch for portfolio. For your presentation sketchbook, it is perfect for defining your final cut collection designs. The purpose of the working sketch is to help others visualize your design ideas and how they drape, shape, and fit the body. It should show construction but be simply and quickly sketched, never studied. The creative energy of your working sketches, both figure and flat, should express the attitude and aesthetic of your brand. You may find the working sketch a welcome solution if you struggle with the artistic challenges of fully finished portfolio artwork.

5-27 Renaldo Barnette works each project in his sketchbook, designing on the spot in concept meetings as decisions for collection are made.

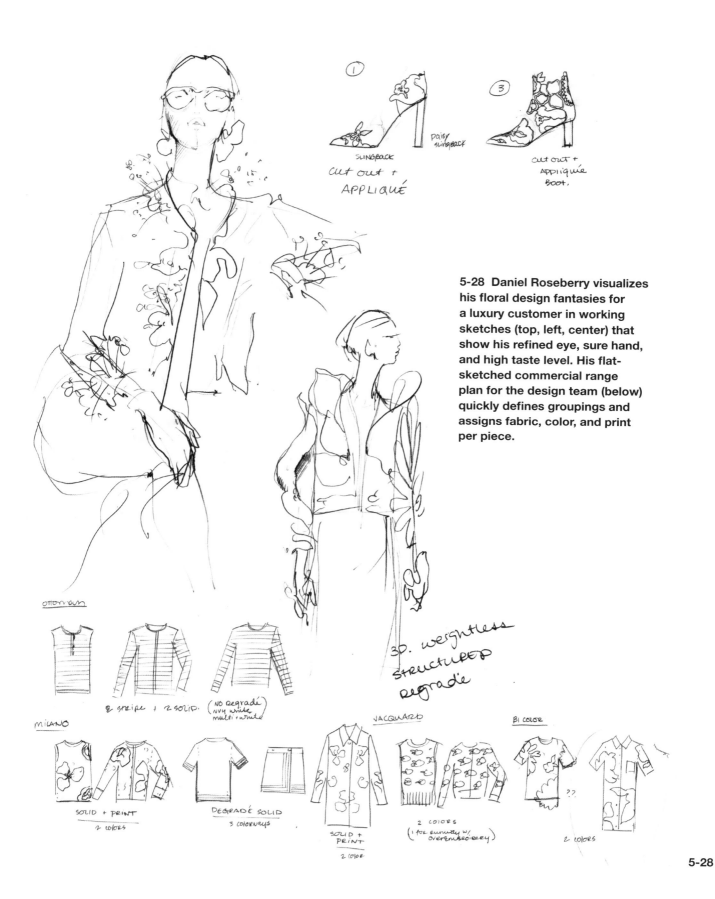

① SLINGBACK

cut out + APPLIQUÉ

Daisy slingback

③ cut out + Appliqué Boot.

5-28 Daniel Roseberry visualizes his floral design fantasies for a luxury customer in working sketches (top, left, center) that show his refined eye, sure hand, and high taste level. His flat-sketched commercial range plan for the design team (below) quickly defines groupings and assigns fabric, color, and print per piece.

OTTOMAN

2 STRIPE + 2 SOLID.

(NO REGRADÉ)
NVY white
multi + white

3D. weightless structured regradé

MILANO

SOLID + PRINT
2 COLORS

DEGRADÉ SOLID
3 COLORWAYS

JACQUARD

SOLID + PRINT
2 COLOR

2 COLORS
(1 for runway w/ overembroidery)

BI COLOR

??

2 COLORS

5-28

5-29

5-29 Renaldo Barnette's presentation sketches communicate attitude and brand aesthetic. Working in water-based brush marker and black Prismacolor pencil, he captures high-fashion proportion and the feel of luxury fabric in elegant, uncomplicated style.

Renaldo Barnette demonstrates this sketch in his video interview online at www.bloomsbury.com/rothman-fashion-sketchbook

Working Sketch Communication

In the design studio, the working sketch is used to communicate your design ideas to colleagues. For initial concept meetings, working sketches, along with visual research, fabric, and color ideas, are combined on team concept boards with visual research and design rationale, worked upon and edited over—and often never make it to the semifinals. Several designers may be contributing their ideas to the mix, and you want your designs to be chosen, so it is important to show that you know design construction and have the ability to draw garment detailing correctly. Sketching your design ideas clearly with attitude, proportion, and style should be automatic. The more comfortable and confident you are with your working sketch, the easier it will be for you to promote your ideas.

Hallmarks of the Working Sketch

- Pose clearly shows silhouette, design lines, and attitude.
- Stylizing creates taste level and expresses muse, theme, and season.
- Sketch is outlined to retain silhouette in fine-tip marker or black pencil.
- Partial rendering is used to quickly suggest color and fabric texture/print in your choice of art supply.
- Construction and garment detailing are lightly but accurately indicated.
- Cropped figures provide close-up views, especially for brief garments.
- Hand-drawn flats accurately match figure sketch designs in construction, proportion, and detail.
- Fabric swatches and descriptive callouts always accompany the sketch.

5-30 Renaldo Barnette—working sketches drawn in Prismacolor pencil.

5-30

Note Buttons

Fine Cotton Voile
Dress w
"Raw Self
Ruffle Detail
& Cotton Organza
Underskirt

Solid
Rayon
Matte Jersey
"One-sy"
w/
Contrast
Zippers

Renaldo Barnett

5-31

5-31 Renaldo Barnette sketches market-influenced variations on working sketch figure proportion and attitude according to price point and brand-specific customer ideals: high fashion; career; young and trendy.

Styling Working Sketch Proportion and Attitude

Design and silhouette should be your first consideration in choosing your working sketch pose. An exaggerated pose or gestures will distort the proportion, shape, and detail of your designs. So whether drawing freehand or using your own figure template, stylize your design surface with a simple, relaxed stance and balanced movement, using body attitude and sketch technique to communicate aesthetic. With your focus on the figure's design surface, the head, hands, and feet should be minimal and support the look. Stylizing a sketch means knowing which lines to leave out and which are absolutely essential to tell the design story of this look in this sketch. This is the art of it—perfected over time and with experience. As you draw fashion proportion, fit, and silhouette on a daily basis, you will lose your conscious attention to the individual elements of the sketch and, as with Renaldo Barnette, embody your experience automatically in your lines.

Market Influenced Variations on Working Sketch Proportion, Pose, and Attitude

- High fashion/chic: Small head/sleek hair, bone structure evident, long neck, strong shoulder, long rib cage, slim hips, relaxed confidence, elongated legs, fluid movement
- Mid-level/career: Average ideal head, hair styled in trend, fashion proportions with curves evident, muscles toned, long legs, and straightforward, confident stance
- Young/trendy: Larger head, trendy hair, rounded face structure and eyes, small bust, neck and waist and legs are shorter, cute or edgy attitude

5-32 Yolande Heijnen's working sketches personify the trendy, young brand image of Joe Fresh and inform production teams overseas.

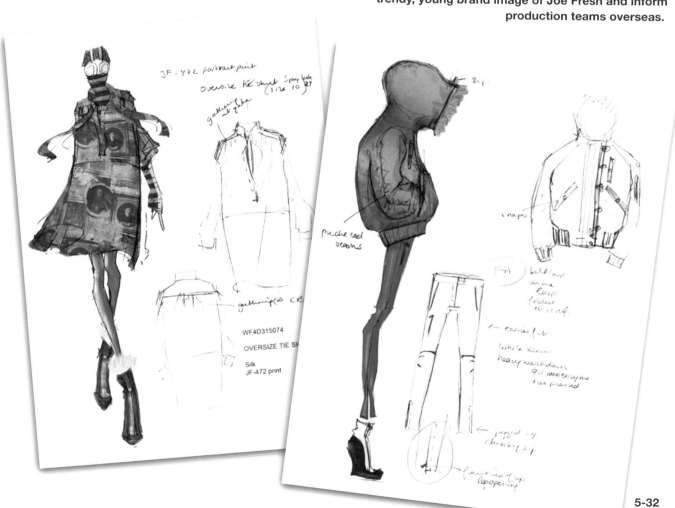

5-32

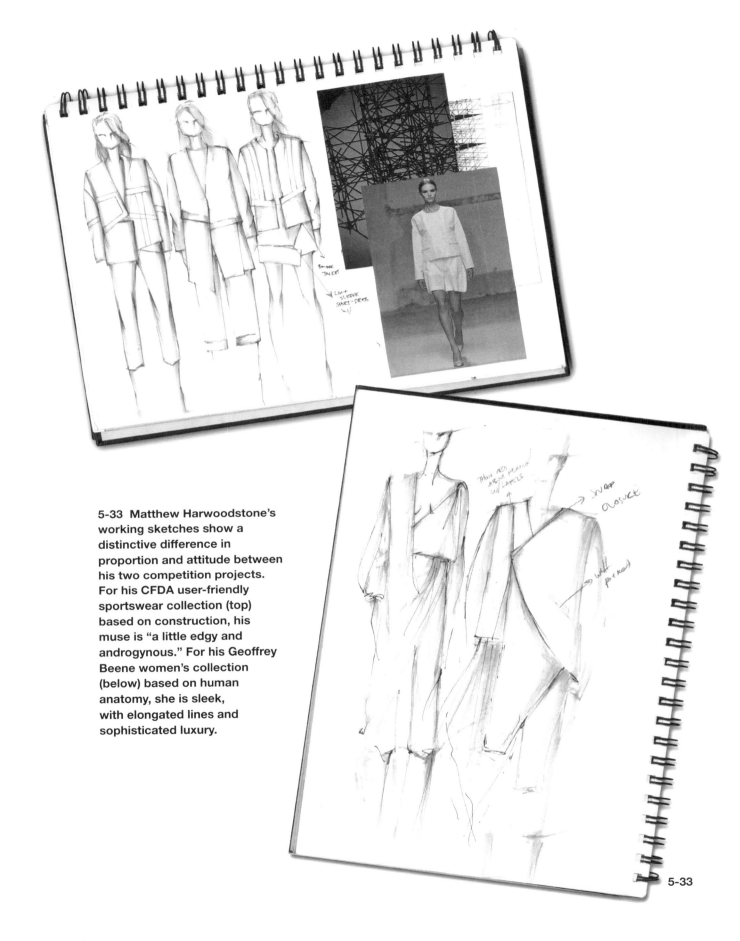

5-33 Matthew Harwoodstone's working sketches show a distinctive difference in proportion and attitude between his two competition projects. For his **CFDA** user-friendly sportswear collection (top) based on construction, his muse is "a little edgy and androgynous." For his Geoffrey Beene women's collection (below) based on human anatomy, she is sleek, with elongated lines and sophisticated luxury.

5-33

5-34 We can see the full evolution of Alexis Chung's avant-garde design grouping through each step in the process for her Art Specialization portfolio collection—initial development (bottom) to working sketch (center) to expressively rendered presentation sketch (right).

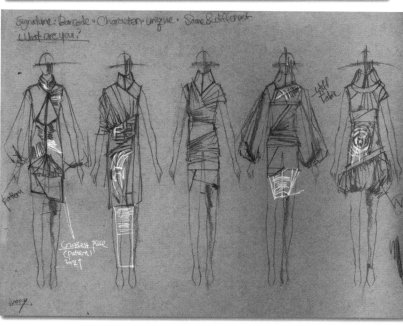

5-34

There is a factual part to a design sketch and an emotional part, and you need a balance of the two. Always react emotionally to a garment or design before you draw it. Your sketch may be completely accurate, but if it is without feeling it can only be good—it can never be fabulous.

—*Steven Stipelman, fashion illustrator, teacher, author*

Minimizing Your Sketching Challenges

Style is a distinctive quality of originality and, like your design philosophy, is always in development. Your sketching style is a matter of individual, personal expression, but never an excuse for drawing out-of-proportion figures, or for sketches that are out of sync with your customer and market. Your style comes from your emotional reaction, and if you try to adopt someone else's style, you can't express or perfect your own. Your way of putting your ideas across may be the right vibe for this moment.

What if your sketching style or skill doesn't yet match your design aesthetic and taste level? After months of experimentation and frustration, Lauren Sehner (see page right) took stock of her best abilities—her high taste level and intuitive design aesthetic. She adapted her sketch style into an expressionist version of fashion style that minimized everything but the design surface of the body. The result was a look perfectly in sync with her minimal sculptural aesthetic and culturally aware, upscale customer. Style very often evolves as you find your own individual solutions to common sketching challenges and incorporate them into your drawings.

5-35

5-36 Lauren Sehner perfected her first working sketch figures into a finished portfolio sketch style that expresses her design aesthetic.

5-36

5-35 and 5-37 Gayoung Ahn's mix of pattern and texture comes to life in the sequential rhythm of her working sketch design variations in final edit.

5-37

5-38 Luba Gnasevych (above) employs cropped figures to emphasize key collection looks; varying figure size creates visual rhythm and interest. Kieran Dallison demonstrates his creative process and sketching talents, from initial color and sequence ideas (below left) to working sketch designs (below right) to final process presentation sketch (center left).

EXERCISE 13: Process Sketch to Working Sketch

Page Layout/Visual Direction

- Target a grouping of your final cut process sketches for this exercise.
- Using spatial dynamics, experiment by sketching a few different double spread layouts that integrate theme imagery and fabric with your working sketches.
- Create an interesting flow, emphasizing key design(s) for the grouping.
- Figures can be enlarged and cropped; zoom diagrams can be added.
- Plan your design direction words and callouts.

Sketch Technique

- Draw working sketch versions of your process sketches, taking care that proportion, silhouette, and detail stay true to your original designs.
- Sketch freehand or use figure templates, resizing when needed.
- Preserve the spontaneous quality of your aesthetic sketch style.
- If you sketch in pencil, define your sketches lightly in fine-line pen; working on tracing paper for professional sketches is not recommended.
- Indicate color, texture, and print and add accurate construction and detailing with a light hand.
- Attach fabric swatches for each garment.
- Stylize your muse with attitude; add seasonal accessories, hair, and makeup.

> As you visualize the conceptual thread running through your design story . . . chart how your pages will work together in sequence. "

Sequencing Plan

A sequencing plan is an essential step in ensuring continuity for any multipage presentation, such as look book or e-portfolio. It helps you create a continuous flow from page to page as you visualize the conceptual thread running through your design story. Way-finding elements connect the dots of visual energy in your sketchbook presentation with titles, labels, repetition of associated imagery, and graphic continuity. They also act as content markers and identify what your viewer is seeing—season, theme, and design vision. Experimenting with spatial dynamics and graphic strategies has given you the tools to understand and control the flow of your sketchbook content as you create it. But you need a visual overview to chart how your pages will work together in sequence.

5-39

Scott Nylund demonstrates pencil-rendering techniques for this figure in his video interview online at www.bloomsbury.com/rothman-fashion-sketchbook

Charting Presentation Flow

If you haven't already sketched a few layout ideas, plan your sequence of pages now. Combine them into a rough visual outline or flow chart of double spreads as you want them to appear in your sketchbook presentation, with each page containing the content you imagine will best serve your story. With the visual flow in front of you, it is much easier to edit and remix as you like, trying out several options until you get what you want. I could not have put this book together visually without the use of a sequential page-planning template. I highly recommend sketching out a thumbnail-sized double spread template, in multiple copies, to help you visualize your sequence. They can be rough sketches, but *do make sure your format size is in correct proportion to your actual sketchbook pages.* (See Peter Do's plan, next page.) As you work out your presentation sequence, think beyond the sketchbook and use it for experimental planning for your portfolio. Some designers also make an actual half-size mockup, or "dummy book," using copy paper stapled together. They rely on it for sketching in their page sequence trials to refer back to as they produce their final version.

5-39 Scott Nylund starts with a rough visual plan to guide his design direction and project overview. For this project, he used his travel diary for "thoughts, ideas, and visual inspiration I stumbled across in my journey through Peru." His original source research includes organic beading, embellishments, and fabric swatches found at local markets, which sparked further sketchbook development, presentation planning notes, and the beginnings of his finished art.

5-40 "These are just two of my thumbnail spreads (below) from the hundreds I sketched when charting the visual flow of this book." —Sharon Rothman

5-40

5-41 and 5-42 Peter Do interprets color and page design from the artist who inspired his collection (top left), carrying it through the run of pages for his formal competition presentation (opposite page). His sequential plan sketch (below) made it possible for him to judge whether his design flow was cohesive and aesthetically connected throughout.

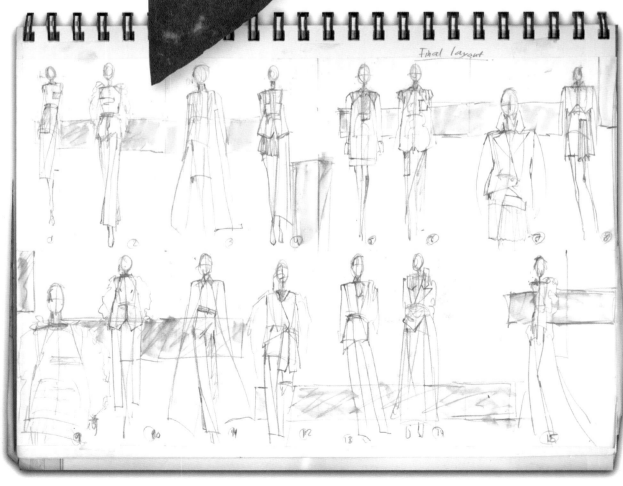

5-41

EXERCISE 14: Presentation Sequencing Plan

- List what you intend to place on each page.
- Sketch out a rough, double spread template in correct thumbnail page proportion to be copied and reused for trial placements.
- Check that all your essential elements, touchstone visuals, and working sketch layouts are at hand.
- Create a visual outline for your content placement, charting how you intend to lay out your pages in sequence.
- Utilize visual direction to create content movement and sequential continuity through your sketchbook pages.
- With your sequencing plan overview in place, judge the flow of your process to match your market and aesthetic.

5-42

After moving to the United States from Vietnam in 2004, Peter Do attended FIT, receiving the Art Specialization Critic's Award in 2012, top honors in the 2013 CFDA Scholarship competition, and an Honorable Mention in the Geoffrey Beene Scholarship competition. His BFA thesis collection was selected as an FIT Critic Award winner in 2014, and upon graduation he was awarded the prestigious inaugural LVMH Prize for Young Fashion Designers, which launched his career with a one-year contract with the LVMH fashion house Celine.

5-43

PETER DO

" I want my sketchbook always to be about what I'm feeling at the moment, how I'm inspired by the composition and shapes of what I see. "

You design intuitively . . . do you work with a design direction for collection?

As I begin, I like to give myself guidelines or basic rules to follow, so I don't stray away from what I want out of a certain collection. For my CFDA collection, I went back to the basic silhouettes. I was inspired by the composition, shapes, and layering of artist Benjamin Carbonne, who paints like I would love to paint if I was a fine artist. My main goal was to make womenswear that is inspired by menswear. I wanted to do something very personal, a blending of artistic vision and clothes that are wearable and marketable.

Do you challenge yourself as you design?

Yes, for this collection I wanted to turn the essentially menswear white shirt into something new. As I was experimenting, I developed a technique that completely transformed the texture of fabric and leather. Using Carbonne's paintings as print, I manipulated scale and image, enhanced brushstroke, and then used innovative transfer techniques onto fabric and leather. To bring other layers to the collection, I widened my focus from technology and went back to craftsmanship, artisanal techniques, and textural knit swatches.

Your sketchbook embodies all of these techniques . . .

For my cover, I hand-painted leather in the same technique I used throughout the whole collection. As I collaged images from the paintings with my process sketches, I used my own kind of brushstroke painting and borrowed elements of color from his palette to make it meaningful. Adding the printed swatches, it all blends into one significant mood page that is more than just simple images.

How do you approach your sketchbook process?

I want my sketchbook always to be about what I'm feeling at the moment, how I'm inspired by the composition and shapes of what I see. For me, the colors can't be random . . . they have to come from somewhere meaningful. I spend a lot of time on developing my fabrics and that is an important part of my sketchbook—to show something different in my process. When it comes to quick sketches, I usually use croquis for whatever I think the silhouettes ask for. I just put it down really quick, and then add notes to show what I'm thinking.

See Peter Do's video interview and sketchbook tour online at www.bloomsbury.com/rothman-fashion-sketchbook

5-44

5-44 Peter Do—presentation sketch for the CFDA Scholarship competition in acrylic paint, fine-tip black marker, and white gel pen on kraft paper.

5-45

KIERAN DALLISON

Kieran Dallison brought design intuition with him from Arizona to New York City for his BFA in fashion design. In 2011, he became the first FIT competitor to win the top prize in womenswear in the CFDA Scholarship program and was concurrently awarded the CFDA/Gilt All-Star Scholarship in 2012. He interned with Prabal Gurung and The Row and, upon graduating, transitioned into a career with iCB in spring 2012. He is currently the associate designer at Altuzarra.

What is the best design advice you received as an undergraduate?

Our fantastic critic, Mark Waldrop, took a red Sharpie to my super-finessed under-drawings and began to regroup them, changing the positions of legs and heads to create a more cohesive layout. I was traumatized! But in doing that, he immediately taught me to think in a unit, think with an end result in mind. It was hard to take, but actually, that visual advice has turned into a very useful design tool for me.

5-46 Kieran Dallison—process sketch in lead pencil; final edit working sketch in marker.

5-4

Looking at your thesis sketchbook two years later, what is your reaction?

There is something so exciting about the spontaneous sketches, which I didn't appreciate when I did them. At the time, the push was toward very clean, crisp digital projects, but there was no sense of real feeling there, or of the work that went into making them. But these sketches are the authentic drawing, an immediate step . . . and somehow they breathe more.

When hiring, what do you look for in a sketchbook?

Spontaneous, imperfect pages . . . Words on the pages tell me you are thinking and that your work is genuine. When putting together images with sketches, keep in mind that everyone has a Tumblr account or can do a Google image search, and there is a saturation point with images. So, rather than putting the images forward on the page, the importance should be on the sketch.

See Kieran Dallison's video interview and sketchbook tour online at www.bloomsbury.com/rothman-fashion-sketchbook

5-47 Kieran Dallison—presentation sketches in marker with white brushstroke texture.

5-47

The world is moving so fast these days that the man who says it can't be done is generally interrupted by someone doing it. 99
—*Elbert Hubbard*

CHAPTER 6

INNOVATIVE/INTERACTIVE SKETCHBOOKS

Each succeeding generation brings a fresh vibe to the creative fields, changing the way we see and do things—inspired by the past, innovating off the best of new technologies, and inventing possibilities for all of us. Your goal is always to be relevant in today's design environment and have the foresight and flexibility to recognize and incorporate change as it happens—and, for many of you, to create that change. The telling of your design story becomes central to sustain design going forward, and like reading tea leaves, your creative process shows us what the face of change will look like.

The electrifying thing about change is the anticipation of where it will take us. Young designers around the globe, each in their own way and with their individual aesthetic, are evolving a portfolio of the future—one that combines a mix of accomplished skills with raw creative process. They are changing the fashion formula by succeeding at designing small and attracting the women who wear their clothes with a more personal connection to the designer's process. When faced with challenge, they do what designers do best: put old ideas and techniques together with new, expediently and with fresh vision—coming full circle by connecting. They are digging in, taking risks in the marketplace, and independently choosing to reconnect with authentic design, and each other, to create a sustainable future.

6-1

6-1 Peter Do's gritty translation of design story for his winning CFDA competition sketchbook reflects a blending of European conceptual expression, Asian design sensibility, and American pragmatic ingenuity.

6-2 Finalist Traci Reed reconnects old techniques with new vision and graphic clarity for her CFDA Scholarship competition sketchbook presentation.

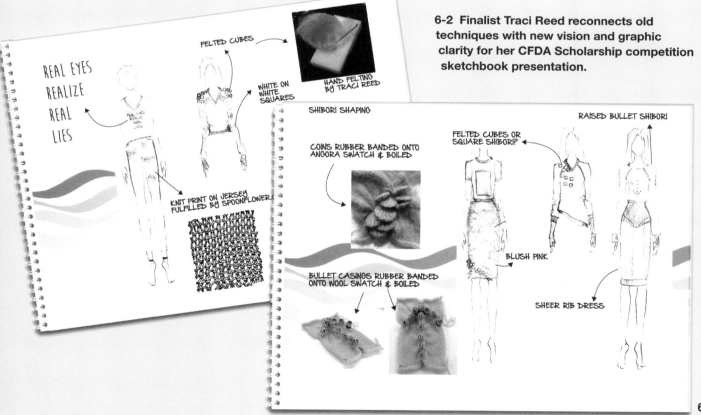

REAL EYES REALIZE REAL LIES

FELTED CUBES

WHITE ON WHITE SQUARES

HAND FELTING BY TRACI REED

KNIT PRINT ON JERSEY FULFILLED BY SPOONFLOWER

SHIBORI SHAPING

RAISED BULLET SHIBORI

COINS RUBBER BANDED ONTO ANGORA SWATCH & BOILED

FELTED CUBES OR SQUARE SHIBORI?

BLUSH PINK

BULLET CASINGS RUBBER BANDED ONTO WOOL SWATCH & BOILED

SHEER RIB DRESS

6-2

It's like an entire generation of people facing forward, but looking back . . . It inspires me!

—*Kristian Bush,* The Bush Brothers, *Turner Classic Movies*

The Elements of Invention

Each sketchbook is an entirely individual mirror on the world, which is being reshuffled by technology and galvanized by global community. For some of you, this comes from being fortunate enough to live in and learn from another culture or from connecting with the lineage of craft through artisanal handcrafting. For others, it springs from intuiting the moment, absorbing it in a personal way, and reflecting it in the creative process. Young Europeans are modifying design fantasy with practicality in their sketchbooks, while young American designers are including more conceptual design associations.

The perfectly rendered fashion illustration and the digitally slick presentation now seem out of sync with the seismic shift toward real clothing and authentic design. We are called to be conscious in our design—of craft, performance, and the lives of the people who wear it. The portfolio of the future will showcase a more authentic storytelling of design that escapes the plastic sleeve onto a real, touchable page, with texture, dimension, and cleanly curated visuals placed in context with sketched design.

6-3 Lauren Sehner: Senior thesis portfolio, "Composite" fall/winter collection.

COMPOSITE

LAUREN SEHNER

6-3

6-4 Alejandra Sevilla: CFDA Scholarship competition, special occasion collection journal.

To reinvent a portfolio for this moment, look no further than your sketchbook. If you are a perfectionist in your artwork, try switching your lovingly rendered figures into loose sketchbook-style pages, as Alejandra Sevilla does. By contrasting perfection with process, her designs become more alive. Her viewers can judge at a single glance whether she will be a good fit for their design team.

Creating balance in any presentation shows design confidence and advances your work. If your sketching is rough or your style is not where you want it to be, try packaging your figures as if they were abstract gems in a cleanly designed graphic setting, with market-smart, merchandized flats and clear concept visuals. Lauren Sehner excels in the sketchbook-portfolio merge for her senior thesis, introducing a clear visual connection between her initial process and finished designs. She tells her concept story through balance, visual metaphor, and spatial dynamics.

The Process Portfolio

We see a new vision for portfolio in the work of innovative young New York City designer Lauren Sehner, who responded to the challenges of her senior thesis collection presentation with the radical idea of combining sketchbook with portfolio. It saved time and solved the puzzle of how to visually connect her original thinking into a polished design narrative. Lauren used her sketchbook for graphic layout trials and as a resource—it was all there for her but the polish. Moving whole chunks of visual associations and page development from her process sketchbook, she integrated them into a concise design story with freshly rendered final sketches, a few flats, and diagrams. By adding tactile, handcrafted elements, a strong title page, and a concise design statement, she brought her design message into clear focus.

 An interview process is so short that if you don't grab your audience right away, you've lost. So putting your process into your portfolio makes sense . . . they can see everything at once.
—Lauren Sehner

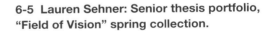
6-5 Lauren Sehner: Senior thesis portfolio, "Field of Vision" spring collection.

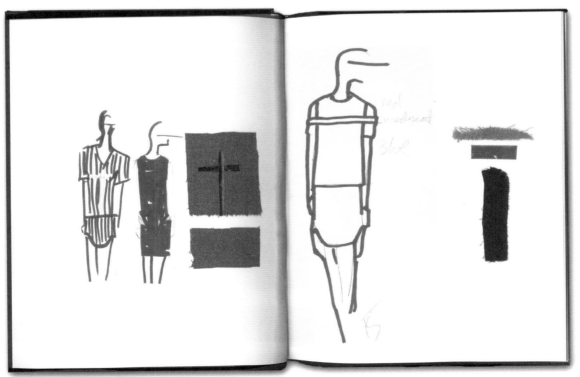

6-5

6-6 How to communicate a design concept in four sequential images: "For my fall 'Composite' collection, I explored the technique that modernist furniture designers use, creating innovative shapes by applying heat to plywood. By translating it to wool felt, I created elegant forms using minimal seams." —Lauren Sehner

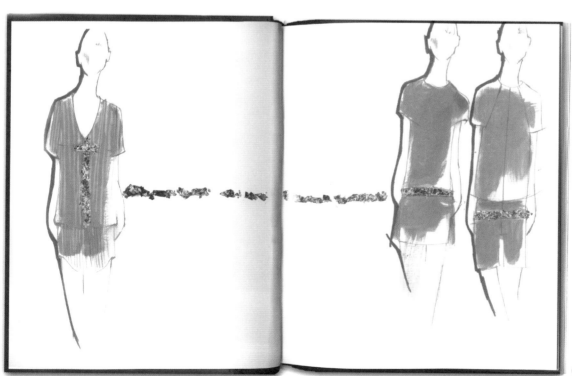

6-7 Lauren Sehner: Senior thesis portfolio, "Field of Vision" spring collection.

Sketchbook Portfolio

In a presentation sketchbook that could pass for portfolio, Matthew Harwoodstone excels in meeting the demands of a major scholarship competition brief designed to extract the essence of a candidate's process. His bold design concept employing folded shapes is suggested in his surreal reworking of anatomical photo images. He makes his design associations easy to see by juxtaposing them with a mix of development and stylized working sketches clear enough to substitute for finished drawings. Matthew's presentation demonstrates sophisticated concept, shape-driven design ideas in development, sharp editing, and knowledgeable construction—communicating aesthetic and vision all in one go.

6-8, 6-9 and 6-10 Matthew Harwoodstone: Geoffrey Beene Scholarship competition finalist, 2014.

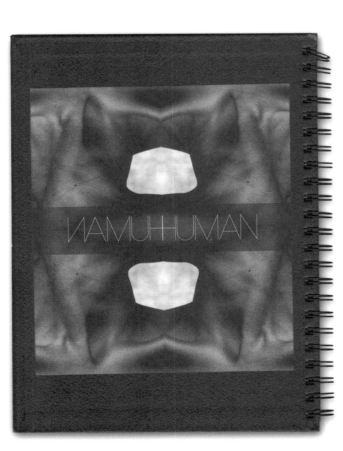

6-8

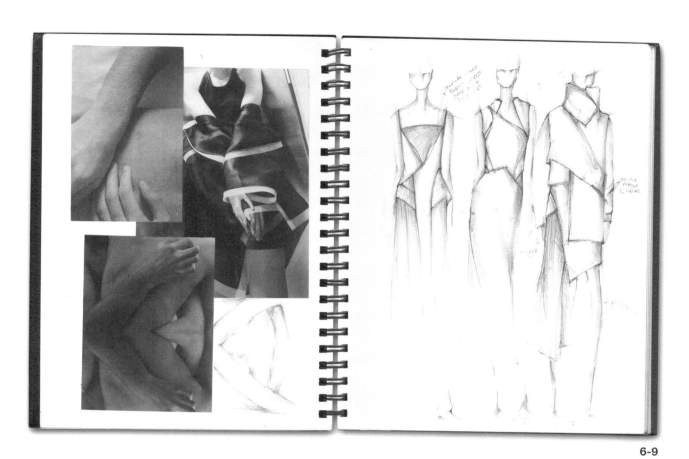

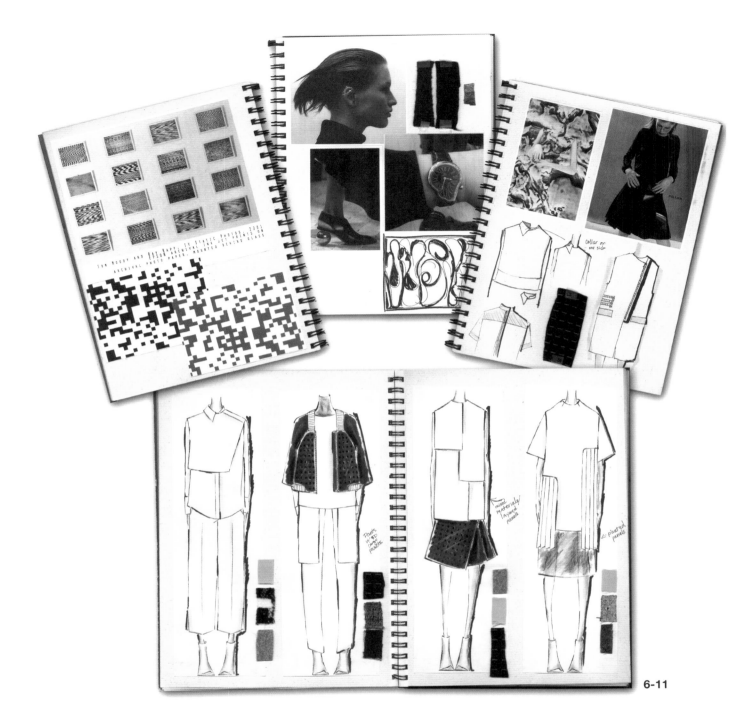

6-11

Sketchbook Portfolio Techniques

Sarah Conlon mastered the art of visual storytelling in her senior thesis sketchbook, designing for a young contemporary customer. Here she presents the whole aesthetic package and stays true to concept, from idea to well-realized designs that are both inventive and wearable. All this is evident in the confidence of her hand, the message of her design thinking, and a clean, professional presentation that marries process with fresh, skillfully finished looks—no portfolio necessary.

See Sarah Conlon's sketchbook tour video online at www.bloomsbury.com/rothman-fashion-sketchbook

Los Angeles designer Sonja Nesse's experience in mainstream brand launch design and designer–retail partnerships has influenced the streamlining of her creative process. Her sketchbook is the "living document" of her design thinking, recording her process from pin board to a sketchbook portfolio that is digitally calibrated to look its best in smart device viewing. After scanning her quickly hand-sketched designs, Sonja selects color from mood images, editing in trial sequences. To achieve a freshly hand-rendered look in her finished groupings, she uses a combination of computer techniques, making adjustments for online viewing. Readable notes and casual fabric swatches lend a sketchbook feeling and textural dimension. Sonja's sketchbook portfolio allows her to share her design vision and process online and on tablet.

Read Sonja Nesse's interview at the end of this chapter.

6-11 and 6-12 Sonja Nesse relies on her sketchbook for continual experimentation. It acts as a springboard for taking her quick design sketches to the next level via computer techniques, as shown below, for a more polished sketchbook portfolio calibrated for smart device viewing.

6-12

6-13 Surrounded in her studio by her sketchbook process wallboards, Luba Gnasevych designs and drapes each collection off of her own carefully chosen directional images and sketched ideas.

The Studio Sketchbook

Many designers use their studio walls as an extension of their sketchbook to develop their designs in the way that feels easiest and most organic for them. All the elements of process are there. Each individual's creative box has grown with experience, expanding the sketchbook beyond page boundaries.

Luba Gnasevych designs downtown clothes for the "edgy, urban, cool girl" in her New York City fashion district studio. She is "always sketching ideas and inspiration" in a small book she carries with her as she shops and sources fabric. She collects inspiring images online, switching them on or off her studio wallboard as the mood strikes her. When starting a collection, she is surrounded by her selected images and color and fabric direction, along with sketches developed directly from ideas and draping trials. She focuses her thinking into concept and design in a larger studio sketchbook, adding her sketches to the wall for editing and final sequencing.

Sunghee Bang's tiny studio in Brooklyn is full, floor to ceiling, with irresistible colors and yarns, hand-knit stitch trials, and design sketches for her current collection. It's like sitting inside her sketchbook. She loves the creative challenge in developing knitwear, which requires her to envision her collection based solely on yarn quality and understanding its characteristics. As she experiments with knit constructions and silhouettes, the details are constantly changing, leading to new creative directions. Sunghee starts a season early, choosing the yarn combinations and inventing stitches that might become her silhouettes, adapting one to the other as they develop and editing as she goes. Her sketches emerge out of this process and are then used to plan and merchandise her collection. She has sought out and nurtured a creative relationship with local hand knitters whose skills, productivity, and friendship support her work in return.

Read Sunghee Bang's interview at the end of this chapter.

6-14 Sunghee Bang creates unique hand-knit designs under her own label, organizing her direction and process for each collection on the walls of her studio, where they guide her intuitive sense of shape and color.

SUNGHEE BANG

6-14

Between the shop and my brand, I'm using different sketching apps and tools on a daily basis. It really speeds things up for me.

—Angélique Chmielewski

The Smart Device Sketchbook

For Brooklyn-based Canadian designer Angélique Chmielewski, her tablet has become a direct visual communication device, connecting her with factory and patternmaker. One of the apps she uses, Noteshelf, transforms her tablet into a smart sketchbook of sorts, allowing her to quickly ease through language barriers by sketching ideas, revising designs on the screen, and sending them instantly.

"It's indispensable for sending Pantone color specs directly to the manufacturer," says Angélique. "I no longer need to send packages overseas . . . it can all be done by email." She uses her tablet sketchbook app when editing and develops colorways via the toolbar brush palette, shown opposite. Using a stylus or her fingertip, she can rethink color or design and instantly visualize it in her sketched line-up. To integrate draping trials, she takes tablet snaps into the app program and draws directly over the screen photo, trying out changes in seam lines or detailing, then sends it to herself for further work in Photoshop. Although app sketches can be very spontaneous, their accuracy doesn't serve her for sketching out a collection. She says, "There's nothing quite like doing it by hand. Otherwise it feels like there's something missing in my process."

ANGÉLIQUE CHMIELEWSKI

6-15

6-15 Angélique Chmielewski.
Photograph by Stephanie Noritz

6-16 Angélique's smart sketchbook process includes visualizing color and fabric on her hand-sketched designs and making on-the-spot editing changes.

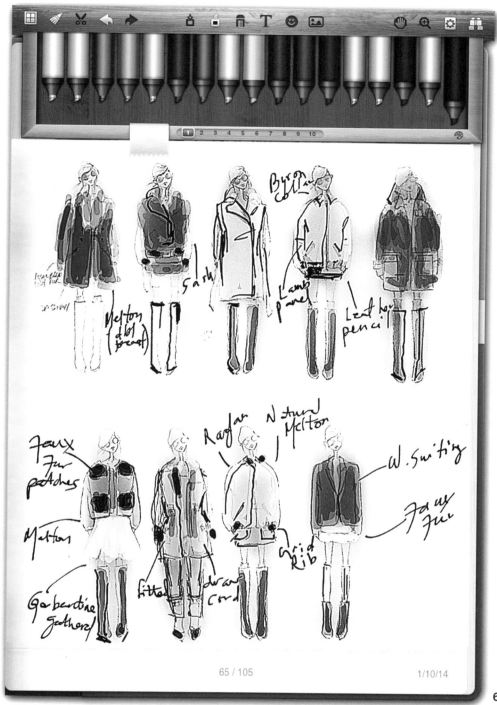

6-16

In response to an increasingly e-world, people are looking for old-world skills and quality materials as well as design innovation. Your design process is what sets you apart. Keep it real and intact by aiming your creative standards high and, like Angélique, finding a balance between expedience and your authentic design process.

Designing a Sustainable Future

The living language of design grows by shedding whatever doesn't fuel creative thinking and evolves by absorbing and inventing new ideas every day. You experience it in the sketchbook process—taking in and focusing ideas, editing out what doesn't work, trying new things and reinventing old, challenging your resourcefulness, and communicating your vision. All are qualities you need to effect change and sustain a creative life. It is not always easy to make your way in fashion. Goals must be set with ardor and commitment. Your sketchbook process helps forge your vision into commitment and sets you in the right direction for sustaining your creative future.

6-17 Daniel Silverstein initiated his "Piece Project" as a creative solution to fulfilling his goal of zero waste, with the challenge of creating garments using only the fabric remaining from collection production.
Photograph by Maeghan Donohue

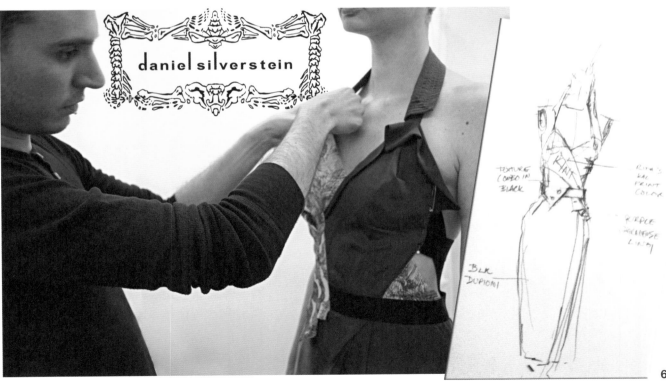

6-17

> **Ours is a living, growing language . . . that sheds old words and absorbs new ones every day.**
> —*Gerald Di Pego, screenwriter*

Conscious Design

Responsible, conscious design is part of the paradigm shift in fashion and systems in general, and many young designers are actively involved in the change. They are frustrated with trying to fit their vision and creative goals into the existing fashion industry matrix, and many have discovered it's an impossible fit. With ears to the ground, they are independently inventing new ways of working and in the process radically shifting how fashion can be done . . . and, with the help of e-commerce and creative collaboration, changing the system for the better.

Today's independent young designers have taken it back to craft, creating first-hand fashion with a conscience. They are sustaining themselves, the environment, and their industry by effecting change in the way they do things—sourcing local and earth-friendly materials and handcrafts, producing clothes ethically and locally, conducting business transparently, and initiating online sales. In the ocean of mass-produced fashion, consumers are responding to well-designed clothes that seem to be made with them in mind, clothing they can live their life in.

Daniel Silverstein means to "change the way people make clothes," by proving that fashion can be beautiful and successful and still be made responsibly, with respect for skilled labor, opportunity for artisans, and sustainable business practices. Daniel is dedicated to his mission of zero-waste design. As quoted on Ecouterre, "Everything we make is zero-waste or less than one percent . . . and made by hand in the USA." Traditional pattern cutting and sewing techniques produce a lot of wasted material. "Zero-waste means that every time we cut fabric, we use the entire piece in production."

6-18 "Dan" Yongeun Lee

6-18

> **This young century has brought about a moment of reflection and radical change. . . . For the first time, a post-fossil society is emerging, using natural ingredients, offering alternatives and giving us hope for the future.**
> —*Li Edelkoort,* Earth Matters

Fashion at large is readjusting, grounding itself in different sensibilities . . . Mostly it's coming from collaborative groups of friends taking on the enterprise of fashion as a fearless form of self expression.

—*Sarah Mower,* American Vogue, *September 2014*

6-19

6-19 Tara St. James

A New Business Model

Tara St. James is an instrumental voice in designing small, slow, and seasonless for her "ethical contemporary womenswear label," Study NY. Through her conscious commitment to sustainability and outreach to community, she builds awareness

for a new business model that "does not subscribe to the traditional fashion calendar" of two major collections per year. Tara is proof that making fewer pieces monthly and selling directly to the consumer works better for both and brings designer and customer together.

"In NYC, we have an incredible community of designers working in the sustainable realm who are generous, transparent, and open source. It's been very helpful in materials sourcing and vetting manufacturers, funding new suppliers, and just bouncing around ideas." Tara starts her creative process by sourcing and choosing the fabrics she wants to work with. "I use two types of sketchbooks, one with blank pages that I can just doodle on, and I like one with grid paper so I can write on it, mark on it, and then plan out collection logistics."

Daniel Silverstein and Angélique Chmielewski are also taking their individual brands forward by opting out of the fashion calendar. Daniel finds that collection size is not sustaining for small designers. "I'm doing a much better business now by creating my own calendar, keeping my collections small, and expanding sales in e-commerce." Like a growing number of young designers, they attract loyal followers by promoting their brands through social media blogs, style reports, and like-minded retail platforms. They stay close to their customers and are able to survive and grow with less overhead and fewer expenses.

Angélique adds, "Besides cutting back on collection size, I'm working one on one with people, collaborating with small boutiques who have the same kind of ideas as me about how I want my brand to be perceived and what the lifestyle of an individual purchaser should be. It's a better way for everyone to be sustainable, creatively, resourcefully, and financially."

Atlanta-based designer Felicia Barth-Aasen founded her label, Collective 26, on the idea of "keeping everything collaborative and sourced through a community of American artisans." She has shifted away from wholesale and cut out the middleman completely. "I'm building my brand nationally by traveling to meet and sell to my customers through trunk shows and online sales. I'm discovering my design strengths directly from the women who buy my clothes."

6-20 Felicia Barth-Aasen's color working sketch translates her design vision to screen print artisans for Collective 26.
Photograph by Leigh Moose for Side Yard Studios

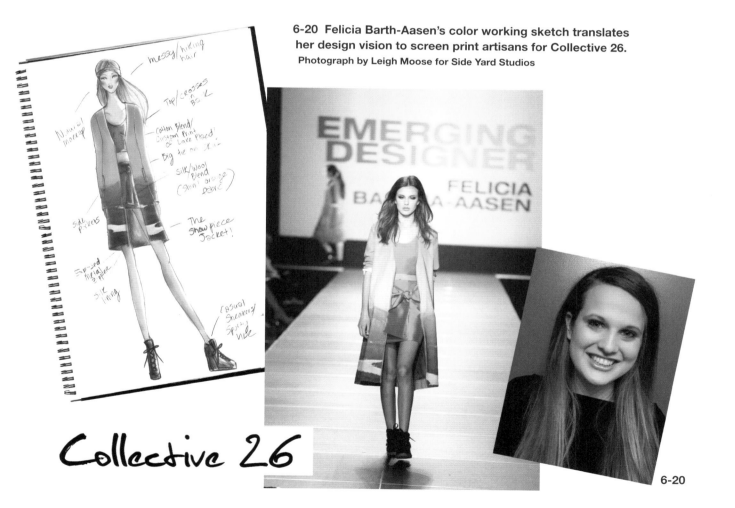

6-20

We want to tell the story behind how and why a product is made, and create a community where both designers and consumers can interact at every level.

—Rosa Ng, founder and creative director, Young and Able

6-21

YOUNG & ABLE

6-21 Rosa Ng, freelance knit designer for Calvin Klein Collection, is a longtime advocate of local and sustainable manufacturing in New York City, concentrating her efforts on her Young and Able design community.

Creative Community

New York City designer Rosa Ng's vision of supporting her friends and design colleagues led her to start Young and Able, a "curated retail platform dedicated to transparency." Rosa has made her niche in e-commerce, bringing creative designers and artisans together with sustainability as a common thread. She invites her online customers into a personal relationship with her product makers. "When you support the designers at Young and Able, you are doing more than just buying their products—you are learning about their inspirations and stories and supporting their future in the industry." Rosa is in a unique position of interface, reading the market and sharing her insights to guide individual designers in making advantageous design decisions. In an openly creative symbiosis, what is best for them is best for her. Their support, friendship, and beautifully crafted goods keep her going in return.

Faced with a present moment that does not easily sustain or support them, young designers on every continent, in urban collectives and regional co-ops around the world, are collaborating with a shared vision and common goals, joining together to support and mentor each other. They are imagining a future based on the creative lineage of design, what worked best in the past, remixed with and developing alongside technology. Their creative community combines small boutiques, local artisans and resources, individual e-shops, and inspired retail platforms—circles of creative friends and colleagues trying out new ways of working together, starting up, and succeeding in the business of fashion—and processing their design inventions by sketching.

Sharon Rothman

6-22 Throughout my long career as a fashion illustrator, I kept my imagination at play and my line quality spontaneous by sketching for fun from a live model whenever possible.

6-22

6-23

SONJA NESSE

After graduating from FIT in 2007, Sonja Nesse got her start in brand development on Vera Wang's design team for Simply Vera, moving on to design on the front end of many different new lines over the next seven years, including Sofia Vergara and Peter Som Design Nation. Sonja has served as independent contributor to trend-forecasting agency Stylesite, and after a recent move from New York City to Los Angeles, she established herself in the role of designer for Reformation.

Is your creative process the same for each line you design?

Yes, I begin my process with research from multiple sources because I'm gathering fuel for the fire. One idea that helps me in my process is to think of my sketchbook as a living document, where nothing is set in stone. I usually work with a pin board, where I can put up my sketches and move things around. As inspirational materials and ideas change and evolve, key concepts start to emerge, and this is where brainstorming really begins for me.

Where does the sketchbook come into your design process?

My direction always goes to sketching first. I have this crazy little sketchbook that I scribble in. When ideas are coming fast, I want to get them down on paper, because one thing always leads to the next. Once I feel complete with that process, I pin the pages on my board where I can step back and see the big picture. At this point, I can drop ideas that are not working, build upon the ones that are, and fill in the missing pieces.

How do you go from development to edit?

Now that my ideas are clear to me, I move on to sketching thumbnails for the collection—complete looks, really fast and messy, but they feel really alive. It's the first time I'm seeing looks I want to work with, which can bring on an epiphany about what I want to include in my final collection. Once I pin them next to the images that inspired them, I see different themes emerge and arrange them in an order that makes sense, one design flowing into the next, until I have a complete story.

See Sonja Nesse's instructive video interview and sketchbook tour online at www.bloomsbury.com/rothman-fashion-sketchbook

6-24

6-24 Sonja Nesse—professional sketchbook color sequence edits for "Still Life" collection: color trials achieved on hand-drawn marker sketches using a combination of computer techniques.

6-25

Sunghee Bang came to New York City from Seoul, Korea, in 2005. While studying fashion design at FIT, she won Critic's Awards in both Knitwear and Art Specializations, apprenticing with New York City designers Donna Karan, J Mendel, Jill Stuart, and Peter Som. In London, she designed several prints for Alexander McQueen's spring 2009 collection. Upon graduating in 2009, she launched her namesake label, focusing on uniquely hand-knit pieces. Her accessory collections are bestsellers at Barney's New York, and in spring 2012, Gen Art selected her collection for their Fresh Faces in Fashion Award.

SUNGHEE BANG

6-26

6-26 Kate Lee—marker sketch

What is your design vision for your label, Sunghee Bang?

My knitwear is characterized by an original approach to surface. I marry minimal silhouettes with intricate textiles, hard masculine qualities with soft feminine touches, craft with high-end design, and sophistication with playfulness. I take an active role in each step of the design process and work with a wide range of materials and knit techniques. I believe that being the key player of the design process retains the strength and individuality of my unique vision.

What do you consider as you develop and edit your ideas into collection?

I work from the idea "unconventional textures with minimal silhouettes." I think about how my designs will function in the life of my customer. I think about offering unique and versatile pieces in the collection and, of equal importance, about efficiency in producing them.

What do you look for in a successful sketchbook?

I think a visual presentation is important for design students. A sketchbook is the best tool to show their thoughts and design process. It's hard to tell which one is successful because it's personal and everyone has different styles. For me, showing knit knowledge is always a plus. But, if I can read their thoughts easily and clearly, I think that is a successful sketchbook.

See Sunghee Bang's video interview and studio tour online at www.bloomsbury.com/rothman-fashion-sketchbook

6-27 Sunghee Bang—knit stitch development sketch in pencil, at left; look book photo of Del Raglan sweater with zoom of knit artistry "perfected by hand."

6-27

RESULCES

RESOURCES

"" **Resources are a designer's treasures.** ""
—Sunghee Bang

4

4 Kate Lee

CHAPTERS 2 AND 3—INSPIRATION/RESEARCH

Museums/Costume Collections

International
—www.fashionandtextilemuseums.com

Metropolitan Museum of Art/Costume Institute, New York, NY
—http://www.metmuseum.org/

The Museum at FIT, Fashion Institute of Technology, New York, NY
—http://fashionmuseum.fitnyc.edu/

Cooper-Hewitt Smithsonian Design Museum, New York, NY
— www.cooperhewitt.org

Los Angeles County Museum of Art (LACMA), Los Angeles, CA
— http://www.lacma.org/

The Royal Ontario Museum, Ontario
—http://www.rom.on.ca

Victoria & Albert Museum, London
—http://www.vam.ac.uk/

The Fashion and Textile Museum, London
—http://ftmlondon.org/

Musée de la Mode et du Textile, Paris, France
—www.lesartsdecoratifs.fr

Musée Galliera, Paris, France
—http://palaisgalliera.paris.fr

ModeMuseum Provencie Antewerpen/MoMu, Belgium
—www.momu.be

Palazzo Pitti Costume Gallery, Florence, Italy
— http://www.polomuseale.firenze.it

Triennale di Milano
—www.triennale.it

Cristobal Balenciaga Museoa, Getaria, Spain
—http://www.cristobalbalenciagamuseoa.com/Ingles.html

Museo del Traje, Madrid, Spain
—http://museodeltraje.mcu.es/

The Kyoto Costume Institute, Kyoto, Japan
—http://www.kci.or.jp/archives/index_e.html

Libraries

Fashion Institute of Technology, Gladys Marcus Library, New York, NY
—http://www.fitnyc.edu/library.asp

New York Public Library, New York, NY
—http://www.nypl.org/
The Picture Collection, Mid-Manhattan Branch
Library for the Performing Arts, Lincoln Center

Fashion Institute of Design and Merchandising Library, Los Angeles, CA
—http://fidm.edu/en/about/FIDM+Library

London College of Fashion Library, University of the Arts, London, UK
—http://www.arts.ac.uk/fashion/about/facilities/lcf-library/

The British Library, London, UK
—http://www.bl.uk/

Bloomsbury Fashion Central/Berg Fashion Library/Fashion Photography Archive
—https://www.bloomsburyfashioncentral.com/

Trend: Style and Color

The Trend Cult
—www.thetrendcult.blogspot.com

Style.com
—www.style.com

WWD/Women's Wear Daily
—www.wwd.com/

The Scene/Vogue Videos
—www.thescene.com/vogue

The Sartorialist
—www.thesartorialist.com

Refinery29
—www.refinery29.com

Business of Fashion
—www.businessoffashion.com

Fashionista
—www.fashionista.com

Trend Union/Edelkoort Inc.
—www.edelkoort.com

Le Book
—www.lebook.com

Color Association of the United States
—www.colorassociation.com

Promostyl
—www.promostyl.com/blog/en/home/

Lenzing Textile (free color, trends downloads)
—www.lenzing.com

Pantone Color Institute/MyPantone
—www.pantone.com

TED
—http://www.ted.com

CHAPTERS 4 AND 5—BIBLIOGRAPHY/SUPPLIES

Bibliography

Albers, J. and N. F. Weber (2013), *Interaction of Color: 50th Anniversary Edition*, New Haven, CT: Yale University Press.

Dawber, M. (2013), *The Complete Fashion Sketchbook*, London, UK: Batsford.

Faerm, S. (2012), *Creating a Successful Fashion Collection*, Hauppauge, NY: Barron's Educational Series, Inc.

Hallett, C. and A. Johnson (2010), *Fabric for Fashion: A Comprehensive Guide to Natural Fibers*, London, UK: Laurence King Publishing Ltd.

Kelley, T. and D. Kelley (2013), *Creative Confidence: Unleashing the Creative Potential within Us All*, New York, NY: Crown Business.

Lupton, E. and J. C. Phillips (2008), *Graphic Design: The New Basics*, New York, NY: Princeton Architectural Press.

Nakamichi, T. (2010, 2011, 2012), *Pattern Magic*, London, UK: Laurence King Publishing Ltd.

Seivewright, S. (2012), *Basics Fashion Design 01: Research and Design*, 2nd edn, London, UK: AVA Publishing.

Shepherd, R. (1995), *Hand-Made Books: An Introduction to Bookbinding*, Tunbridge Wells, Kent: Search Press.

Stipelman, S. (2011), *Illustrating Fashion: Concept to Creation*, 2nd edn, New York: Fairchild Publications, Inc.

Tain, L. (2010), *Portfolio Presentation for Fashion Designers*, 3rd edn, New York: Fairchild Publications, Inc.

White, A. W. (2011), *The Elements of Graphic Design: Space, Unity, Page Architecture and Type*, 2nd edn, New York, NY: Allworth Press.

Wolff, C. (1996), *The Art of Manipulating Fabric*, 2nd edn, Lagos, Nigeria: KP Books.

Magazines—Print and Digital

Vogue Magazine
—www.vogue.com

Self Service Magazine
—www.selfservicemagazine.com

Around the World NYC
—www.aroundtheworldnyc.com

In Fashion/In Trend Magazines
—www.instyle-fashion.com.tw

Hola Fashion
—http://fashion.hola.com/

View Textile
—www.view-publications.com

Cecily Moore's Supply List

X-acto knife

Scissors

Tombow adhesive dispensers, in permanent, removable, and dots

3D Pop Dots

Double-sided tape

No. 2 pencils, HB pencils

Black Sakura Micron pens in sizes 005, 01, 03, 05, and 08

Black Uni-Ball pens

White Sakura Gelly Roll pens

Prismacolor colored pencils

Prismacolor marker (choose sets or individual double-ended markers)

Tombow water-based brush markers

Winsor & Newton Cotman watercolors

Fabriano Studio Watercolor Block in 140 lb and 90 lb

Epson WF-7510 wide format printer and scanner

Cecily's Favorite Online Resources

Adhesives and archival storage:
—http://www.scrapbook.com (international shipping)

For art supplies:
—http://www.dickblick.com (international shipping)
—http://www.jerrysartarama.com (international shipping)
—http://www.greatart.co.uk
—http://www.jacksonsart.com
—http://www.geant-beaux-arts.fr

Art Materials Safety

Art and Craft Safety Guide (download)
—http://www.cpsc.gov//PageFiles/112284/5015.pdf

Kinnally, E. L., Art Materials Safety (download)
—www.pixelatedpalette.com/artmaterialssafety.html

CHAPTER 6—ETHICAL DESIGN COMMUNITY

Ethical Design Research

Not Just a Label
— https://www.notjustalabel.com/

Ecouterre—Eco trends in sustainable fashion, style, and beauty
— www.ecouterre.com

The Green Style Blog
— http://www.vogue.co.uk/person/the-green-style-blog

The Guardian/Sustainable Business
— http://www.theguardian.com/sustainable-business/sustainable-fashion-blog

Gilhart, J., Conscious Consumerism
— www.businessoffashion.com

Hohlbaum, C. L. (2009), *The Power of Slow: 101 Ways to Save Time in Our 24/7 World*, New York, NY: St. Martin's Griffin.

Brown, S. (2010), *Eco Fashion*, London, UK: Laurence King Publishing Ltd.

Ryan, L., The Human Workplace
— www.humanworkplace.com/

Ethical Fashion Forum
— http://ethicalfashionforum.com

Pratt/Brooklyn Fashion + Design Accelerator
— http://brooklynaccelerator.com

Eco Age, the Green Carpet Challenge
— http://eco-age.com/gcc-brandmark/

Clean Clothes Campaign
— https://www.facebook.com/cleanclothescampaign

Ethical Sourcing

Source4Style, eco textile marketplace
— http://www.source4style.com/

Maker's Row (New York City factory sourcing made easy)
— www.makersrow.com

Ethical Fashion Source Network
— http://ethicalfashionforum.ning.com

Fair Trade Foundation
— http://www.fairtrade.org.uk/

Far and Wide Collective
— http://www.farandwidecollective.ca

World Crafts Council
— http://wccna.org/
— https://www.facebook.com/WorldCraftsCouncil
— http://www.wcc-europe.org/

Start Up Fashion
— http://startupfashion.com

EcoSessions
— http://ecosessions.co/

Ethical Online Shops

(connecting ethical designers and conscious consumers)

Young and Able
— http://www.shopyoungandable.com/

Master and Muse
— http://masterandmuse.com/

Modavanti
— https://modavanti.com

Style with Heart
— http://www.stylewithheart.com/

Magnifeco
— http://magnifeco.com

ACKNOWLEDGMENTS

This book was inspired by and written for my students, past, present, and future, whose design ideas and innovative techniques teach me creative possibility and move my design thinking forward. Visuals tell the story of the sketchbook, and I am grateful for and delighted by the creative sketches, sketchbook pages, and personal stories shared by the many former students and colleagues who so generously answered my call for contributions, special interviews, and video demonstrations.

They owe a debt of gratitude, as I most surely do, to the exceptional design ability, intrepid technical skills, and magnanimous spirit of my art editor, Cecily Moore. Thanks also to the gracious videography talents of Claire Franjola, who filmed and collaborated in editing the videos now available for viewing on www.bloomsbury .com/rothman-fashion-sketchbook.

I've learned so much through the process of writing The Fashion Designer's Sketchbook and am grateful to the manuscript reviewers whose thoughtful comments helped me find my voice. I especially thank Colette Meacher, Commissioning Editor/Fashion and Textiles, Fairchild Books UK, for her patient guidance and for supporting and advancing my concept for this book. Thanks to the diligence of Fairchild UK's production team, Claire Henry and James Tupper; to Sutchinda Rangsi-Thompson for her resourceful cover design; to the expertise of Lachina project managers Meredith Hall and Eric Zeiter, and for the skill and flexibility of their team in upholding and sustaining the book's visual flow and aesthetic.

Thanks go to my colleagues at Fashion Institute of Technology, particularly in Fashion Design Art, for being on call and offering material support, friendship, and encouragement. Special thanks to my Art Specialization teaching partner Steven Stipelman, who helped guide my introduction to teaching over twenty years ago. My individual thanks to kindred spirits Josie Vargas, Kathy Strack, Christopher Uvenio, Marie Peppard, Gregory Nato, and in particular to Renaldo Barnette for his inspiring contributions. I'm grateful for generous help from George Simonton, Madeline Orefice, Linda Tain, Michael Casey, and Mary Wilson.

I am delighted and honored to receive endorsements for this textbook from my esteemed colleagues, from design director Daniel Roseberry, and from fashion icon Calvin Klein, benefactor of FIT's Future of Fashion graduate runway show, whose clarity of purpose and design thinking helped inspire this book.

The roots of this book go deep, to my first and most encouraging teachers, my parents. Through my mom's projects and my dad's personal diaries of surveying notes and sketches, sketchbooks came to mean love, independence, and creative ideas. I thank my dear family and friends for being patient and supportive, my sisters Ellen Zappala and Alice McCall, and friends Kristin and Enrique Dura, Patricia Buraschi, Renae Jensen, and Sandra Humby for advice both practical and intuitive. I am especially grateful for the invaluable contributions and trusted experience of Claudine Calabrese, Stephen Joyce, and Martha Morrison.

Keeping me laughing and well fed in the midst of tough book decisions is always my husband, Sol Rothman, creative problem solver and fine artist and writer in his own right. I am forever grateful and ever in love. Thank you for your true design eye and intuitive insights in helping me fulfill my vision for this book.

The publishers would like to thank Tamara Albu, Janice G. Ellinwood, Charlotte Hodes, and Stacey Grant-Canham.

PICTURE CREDITS

Photography Credits

5 Marie Peppard 2014

INDEX